CREATE STORY IDEAS THAT BEG TO BE WRITTEN

THE SIMPLE SECRETS TO START PRODUCING TERRIFIC IDEAS TODAY

JOHN D. BROWN

Create Story Ideas That Beg To Be Written: The Simple Secrets to Start Producing Terrific Ideas Today

Copyright © 2020 by John D. Brown

All rights reserved

Published by Blacksword Enterprises, LLC

This book is licensed for your personal enjoyment only. Except in the case of brief quotation embodied in critical articles and reviews, no part of this publication may be reproduced or transmitted in any form or by any means, electronic or mechanical, including photocopying, recording, or any information storage and retrieval system, without permission in writing from John Brown. Thank you for respecting the hard work of the author.

Cover Design © 2020 Kelli Ann Morgan

ISBN 13: 978-1-940427-25-6 (ebook)

ISBN 13: 978-1-940427-24-9 (paperback)

First edition: January, 2020

Revised July, 2020; October, 2020

❋ Created with Vellum

Join John's Novel Writers Academy newsletter to stay up-to-date with new releases, classes, and receive exclusive content.

www.johndbrown.com

CONTENTS

Start producing ideas that crackle with electricity today ... 1
1. The 3 Things You Must Learn to Write Killer Stories ... 5
2. What's a Story? ... 17
3. Trigger and Delay ... 29
4. The Story Setup ... 34
5. Six Principles that Will Unleash Your Creativity ... 49
6. Compelling Characters ... 72
7. The Character Sketch ... 85
8. Awesome THOMs and Goals ... 101
9. Formidable Obstacles ... 116
10. Don't Turn a Garden Hose into a Snake ... 131
11. Spiderman, Peter Parker, and the Gift of Writer's Block ... 140
12. Interesting Casts ... 147
13. Cool Locations ... 152
14. Multiple storylines ... 156
15. Two Expanded Story Setups ... 161
16. What's next? ... 179

Appendix A: Story Setup Checklist ... 181
Appendix B: Fantasy and Science Fiction ... 185
Dear Reader ... 199
Read More by John D. Brown ... 201
Acknowledgments ... 203
About John ... 205

START PRODUCING IDEAS THAT CRACKLE WITH ELECTRICITY TODAY

Do you want to write novels that make people laugh, cry, wonder, thrill, and sit on the edges of their seats, but find yourself struggling to do that?

Have you read books, watched videos, listened to podcasts, and still just don't get it?

I know the feeling.

I wasn't one of those kids destined to write novels. I didn't emerge from the womb with Shakespeare in one hand and Ernest Hemmingway in the other.

I didn't write my first novel when I was in middle school. Or high school. Or even in college. I didn't put twinkles in my English teachers' eyes.

I didn't even start reading for pleasure until <u>the sixth grade when I discovered *The Hobbit*.</u> And while I read steadily after that, I was not one of those kids who devoured whole bookmobiles. I wish I had been, but I wasn't. Back then nobody would have pointed at me and said, "There. There walks a budding author."

Even so, I loved the novels I did read. I loved them so much that years later, at the end of my second year of college, I finally decided that's what I wanted to do. I wanted to write stories. Stories that, in the

I

words of Emily Dickinson, took the tops of people's heads off. And I figured getting a degree in English literature would teach me how to do it.

Except English literature degrees don't teach you anything of the sort. The name of the degree kind of gives it away. Degrees in English literature are about—you're never going to guess—reading English literature. They are designed to teach you how to critically analyze texts with various literary lenses. What they are not designed to do is teach you how to develop and write stories that whisk readers away on perilous adventures, make their hearts thump with wonderful romance, or scare the soup out of them with tales of suspense and dread.

Yes, my university did offer elective, creative writing classes. In my first one, I wrote a masterpiece that was two paragraphs long and described a moment when I was a water boy, hose in hand, standing outside at my dad's nursery in the hot, Utah summer sun, squirting a stream of water at a grasshopper that had landed on a one-gallon juniper bush.

That was it. Me squirting a grasshopper. Really moving stuff, I know.

But I persisted and took a creative writing class every semester. I did learn some things. And there were parts of my short stories that sparkled every now and again. However, they never felt like the stories I loved.

Even my professors, as wonderful as they were, didn't seem to understand the core of story. I remember going up to one after class and asking him how you knew when to end a story.

He looked at me and said, "I don't know when to end them. I just end them."

What?

And this was a professor who'd published his stories in many literary magazines.

Back then writing was all a vast mystery to me. It seemed you either had it, or you didn't. It was in your DNA, or it wasn't. And as far as I knew there was no instruction on how to put a ripping good yarn together on purpose instead of on accident. Sometimes it felt like it would have been more productive to chase leprechauns.

So, if that's where you are, I know how you feel.

Luckily, over a number of years I had a number of key insights and eventually received a three-book contract from a major publisher. After that, I continued to publish and went on to sell tens of thousands of copies of my novels to readers all across the planet.

And that's why I'm so excited about The Novel Writers Academy because the academy is not about giving you more education *about* writing. It's about pulling the covers off so you can see what's truly at work.

More importantly, it's about you getting trained. With one-on-one help from someone who knows what they're doing. Someone who has written novels, published them, and delighted thousands of readers.

Instead of watching a video or reading a book about writing, you're going to get to work and (1) develop multiple story ideas that beg to be written, (2) create plots that build the type of experiences you love, and (3) write chapters that engage and transport the reader. And you're going to do all of that with one-on-one guidance.

This handbook is meant to accompany the first course, which means that in these pages you'll find all the key concepts, processes, and methods you need to know to support you as you develop the story ideas you'll be working on in class.

For those not taking the course, you will find a wealth of knowledge that you can apply on your own.

However, for those attending the course, you're in for a ride, because you're going to actually apply everything that's here. In fact, when you finish the course, you will leave with a number of ideas that are crackling with electricity. Ideas you yourself developed that are ready for the next step, which is the outline (or your first draft, if you want to try writing by the seat of your pants). The bottom line is that when you finish this first course, you will be a budding, story idea machine.

If you are tired of wandering around in the writing wilderness, you now have a guide in your hand that will help you get to the other side. So let's begin. There are three things you must learn to write killer stories. And that's where we are going to start.

1

THE 3 THINGS YOU MUST LEARN TO WRITE KILLER STORIES

I live up on the hinterlands of Utah. And I mean hinterlands. The closest town has a whopping 248 residents, and I think the number's that high only because they counted a few of the cows.

I'm surrounded by mountains, wide open vistas, and a number of ranches run by men and women who can often be seen riding horses as part of their jobs. Not long ago, after a fine church meeting, I was chatting with one of the ranchers that live here. He asked about my novels and what my latest project was. I described it to him, and then he looked at me, and with a little bit of wonder, said, "I don't know how you do it. Coming up with all those ideas. I could no more do that than fly to the moon."

I smiled and told him that was not true. I said people think writing is mystery. That it's some special gift. But it's not. It's just like any other skill. The problem is that it's not obvious what you need to learn to be successful at it.

"Oh, now," he said, and I could tell he didn't quite believe me.

And so I tried to relate it to his world. I told him I could no more fly to the moon than run a ranching operation like he did. There's a massive amount of knowledge and skill that's required to raise cattle and hay and run and maintain all the equipment. In their arena, these ranchers have more knowledge than any number of PhDs. But was it impossible to learn? Even if I couldn't do it now, was it was possible for someone like me to learn it?

He agreed it was.

I said <u>writing novels is no different. There are certain things you need to learn, and as you learn them you get better and better at it.</u> The key is knowing what you need to learn and whether you are willing to put in the work to learn it.

But what are those things? Well, there are three of them. <u>Three things you must learn to write killer stories</u>:

1. <u>What a story is supposed to do.</u>
2. <u>How the elements of story work together to do that.</u>
3. <u>How to generate options for those elements until you find one that achieves your purpose.</u>

I didn't know any of this when I was first starting out. And that gap in my knowledge was one of the things that held me back for years. In fact, I almost gave up my dream of writing stories because of it. And that was even after I'd had some success.

After years of stumbling around, I wrote a story that won an award and $2,000. I was flown out to Cocoa Beach, Florida for a week-long writing workshop with amazing pros. And then I went home, finished another story, and proceeded not be able to finish another thing for five years.

Five years.

FIVE. FREAKING. YEARS!

And I tried.

After five years of failure you begin to wonder if maybe you were just gaslighting yourself. Your family begins to wonder that as well. You realize life is short and there are a lot of other things you could be spending your time on. You begin to think that only an idiot would spend more time on this. And you'd probably be right.

Unless, of course, you realize that what's keeping you back isn't a manifestation of cosmic will. Rather, it's just a lack of understanding.

Except for some reason we don't think of that. We don't treat writing like we do ranching, or even math. Instead, we treat it as some kind of mysterious gift handed out to rare individuals at birth. But it's not. It's a skill that can be learned just like anything else. And to drive the point home I'm going to call out some of the myths we have about creativity so you can avoid them.

THE MYTHS

There are many of these. Let's look at the top few.

Myth #1: To Be Creative You Must Smolder

Some people imagine that you can only succeed at writing if you are the type that looks at life with a gaze of brooding and smoldering intensity. Such types wear brushed velvet jackets. They usually have rakish, devil-may-care hair. And if they're male, they definitely have a beard.

When you look at such people, you feel the passion radiating off them in waves. Surely, their inner worlds are vast tempestuous seas of passion that send passionate ideas crashing in great surges onto the rocky beaches of their passionate souls. And those passionate forces cannot be contained. No, the artist must write them, write them, write them. They must channel those forces onto the written page because if they didn't, they would surely drown.

"Passionate intensity is the key to creativity."

Except, it isn't.

Sure, you need to be excited about what you write (most of the time), but you don't need to be Mr. or Ms. Smolder. You don't need to wear brushed velvet jackets. I don't know any that do. And you don't need to walk around with an intense, brooding gaze. And while sometimes a gigawatt idea will come to you, I don't know any authors that claim that channeling passion is the secret. What they report, and what I've found, is that it requires work.

Myth #2: If You Don't Smolder, You Must, at the Very Least, Be Eccentric

Fine, some say. <u>Maybe passion isn't necessary, but surely eccentricity is.</u> You need to wear crazy beardage or sit in a big Alice-in-Wonderland chair with funky upholstery when you write. Or maybe, this theory of writing tells us, you can only succeed at writing if you are the type that wears purple pants. Or fancy hats. Or tattoos. Or rides a bike with a pet parrot clinging to the handlebars. Or whatever it is that you might think is eccentric.

<u>But this too is false.</u> Some of the best writers I know are accountants who wear accountant clothes. Others are frazzled moms. Others work in the military and wouldn't be caught dead in purple pants (although many are okay with green).

Okay, fine, you say. But, surely, if nothing else, the hair can help.

Except there are too many *New York Times* bestselling authors who have no eccentric hair whatsoever. There are too many successes that wear regular pants and shirts, sometimes purchased from Walmart.

Myth #3: Fine, Then You Must Have a Certain Personality Type

I remember the day of woe when I took the Meyers-Briggs personality test and learned that I was an ENFJ, and then learned that the "natural" writers were supposedly all ISFPs.

No wonder I couldn't write! Me being a blockhead was all scientific.

	Possible				
NF Valuing					**NT** Visioning
Personal	ENFJ Teacher	INFJ Counselor	INTJ Mastermind	ENTJ Field Marshall	
	ENFP Champion	INFP Healer	INTP Architect	ENTP Inventor	Logical
	ESFP Performer	ISFP Composer	ISTP Operator	ESTP Promoter	
SF Relating	ESFJ Provider	ISFJ Protector	ISTJ Inspector	ESTJ Supervisor	**ST** Directing
	Present				

Meyers-Briggs Personality Grid of Doom

Except this is bogus too.

How can I make such a claim? <u>Because I know writers of all personality types who tell stories that readers love.</u> They're extroverts, introverts, detail-oriented, big-picture-oriented, eccentrics, regular Janes and Joes—you name it.

<u>Writing success doesn't have anything to do with personality type</u>. Don't forget: John Brown was the wrong personality type and yet still managed to figured it out. Hmm.

Myth #4: Okay, Then You Need Certain DNA

This is the three-footed cousin to myths #1, #2, and #3. Sure, you need to have an IQ above that of a rutabaga. But if you meet that bar, you can learn to tell stories.

Another outrageous claim. How can I continue to make such statements?

This one is easy. <u>My assertion rests on the fact that our brains are story-making machines. This is what cognitive science teaches us. Story making is part of what your brain does, every day. It's how we survive. You are constantly making up stories about cause and effect. You are constantly putting yourselves in the other people's shoes,</u> which is why you can feel moments of sympathy, suspense, and joy while watching TV or the neighborhood kid down the street. <u>It's why you learn from the successes and failures of others. Furthermore, you regularly solve problems. Like getting child-proof lids off the tops of bottles. All of this is part of storytelling.</u>

So if you're a human, you've got the DNA. Not only that, it's already turned on and working upstairs.

Myth #5: Then It's Booze (or Weed or Vitamin Supplements)

Some people look at authors like Ernest Hemmingway, who liked his booze, or Lee Child, who it appears smokes whole bushes of marijuana when writing his books, and conclude that normal people can't come up with ideas. They need chemicals to facilitate it.

Except chemical supplementation has nothing to do with it. How do I know? Because I know droves of successful writers who don't use any.

Myth #6, #7, and #8

There are more of these ideas.

There's the one that says in order to be creative you need to be mentally unstable like Vincent Van Gogh.

Van Gogh with stylish beard contemplating comments from his editor

Except, how many one-eared authors do you know?

There's another that says creativity is obtained only as a gift from God.

Create Story Ideas that Beg to be Written

Adam languorously reaching out to touch the Almighty

Well, I guess in a sense this is right because God gave it to all of us—it's in our DNA, remember? So you're blessed, too.

Or there's the idea that to be creative you need to be born to it and manifest it at an early age. Like when you were six. And that if you're over forty, fifty, or sixty, it's impossible to learn.

But how does that theory square with the fact that <u>all of these bestselling authors published their first books *after* they were fifty: Laura Ingalls Wilder, Raymond Chandler, Richard Adams, Frank McCourt, and John Flanagan (who was sixty when his first book was published). Truly, age doesn't matter.</u>

The bottom line is that all of the ideas above about creativity and writing ability are rubbish. Creativity has nothing to do eccentricity, gifts from Odin, or whether you wear Argyle socks.

WHAT CREATIVITY IS REALLY ABOUT

Let me show you the face of creativity.

Warren, Creative Master

That is Warren Ellis. One day our fridge began to fill with water. The freezer would cycle through its normal thawing, and all the water would drip down into the fridge and soak into our egg cartons and pool on the shelves and in the vegetable crispers. It was a mess.

We defrosted the freezer, but the problem persisted. So we called Warren because he fixes things.

Warren came to our house, looked the fridge over, and declared that the freezer's drain tube was plugged. He tried a few things to clean it out, none of which worked, and then Warren asked if we had an air compressor. We did and hauled it into the kitchen.

Warren plugged it in, let it build up the pressure, and then held the compressor nozzle to the bottom end of the tube. The compressed air went in. The obstruction flew up and out and landed on the counter. And we discovered the obstruction was a fat fly that had crawled into the tube, gotten stuck, and died.

We poured a quart of water into that freezer, and it all flowed down into the catch pan at the bottom. Warren fixed our freezer with an air compressor.

What did Warren have? He didn't have passionate hair. No. He had an objective. He knew basically how fridges worked. And he had some methods that let him come up with a couple of options to fix the issue until he found one that worked. He knew the three things required for killer fridge fixes.

Let's look at another example. Here's Ed Smylie.

Ed, Creative Master

Ed was like Warren. He ran into some problems. Actually, the astronauts in Apollo 13 ran into some problems. They were running out of air.

The spacecraft had three modules—a lunar module for landing on the moon, a service module, and a command module which was also the capsule they used to re-enter Earth's atmosphere and splash into the ocean with. The problem was that the oxygen tank in the service module failed two days into the mission. With the oxygen in the service module gone, the only way to get the astronauts back was to move them to the lunar module. But it couldn't filter the carbon dioxide that would build up in the air. To do that they had to move the square carbon dioxide filter cartridges from the command module to the lunar module and get them to work in a totally different system.

Ed and the others designed the solution in two days. The ground crew relayed the instructions to the flight crew. The lunar module's CO_2 scrubbers started working again, saving the lives of the three astronauts on board. Of the experience, Ed said that he knew the problem was solvable when it was confirmed that duct tape was on the spacecraft. "I felt like we were home free", he said. "One thing a Southern boy will never say is: I don't think duct tape will fix it."

Ed and his crew saved the day. They made a round peg fit into a square hole. How did he come up with such a creative solution?

Ed had an objective. He knew how the CO_2 scrubbers and the spacecraft worked. He knew about duct tape. And he had some methods to come up with options until he found one that worked. He knew the three things for coming up with killer fixes to space capsule problems.

Creativity is built into our brains. Some solutions are brilliant. Others make you smile. Like the woman who fixed the broken sideview mirror on her minivan by attaching a large, purple-framed hand mirror to it with hair elastics.

Or the man whose toilet paper holder broke, and so he decided to do this.

A portable roll holder

Or the family who needed a latrine when they went out camping in the wilderness, but didn't want to dig. And so they came up with a hitch-mountable, portable, redneck crapper dubbed the Bumper Dumper.

For those who want to tan while they toilet

What did all of these fine folks have? They had a goal. They knew the basics of how things worked. And they had some method to come up with some potential solutions until they found one that did the job.

That's all there is to creativity. Three things. Not so mystical, is it?

But I can hear some of you complaining. Writing is different. It's a whole other world. It's Fiction, which is so significant we must capitalize it. It's passion. It's mystical. It's a matter of the dark recesses of the mind. It's not a fridge or space ship. You cannot compare these things.

Except I can because the process is the same. It doesn't matter if you're trying to adapt a recipe, decorate your house, come up with a way to keep the squirrels out of your bird feeders, or make people weep while watching a movie. You need to know three things:

- What you're trying to accomplish. — GOAL
- A basic knowledge of how things work in that arena.
- Methods that help you come up with potential solutions until you find one that does the job.

The problem is that new writers don't know what they're trying to accomplish, they don't know how the parts of story work to accomplish those things, and they don't have effective methods for coming up with potential solutions.

No wonder we conclude it's a mystery.

But it just ain't so. You're a human. You have a brain. The type of brain that can come up with a redneck crapper. And that means you can write a story.

Now, it's true that a lot of people feel their way through this. They don't know what they're doing and kind of woo-woo themselves into it. I did that, remember? I won an award. But then I couldn't repeat it. Couldn't find that groove I'd stumbled into.

However, if you're like me, you don't want to stumble around hoping to get lucky. You don't want to write stories on accident. The good news is that you don't have to. You can create terrific stories on purpose because there are principles to invention. When we learn them, our productivity shoots through the roof.

Finding a solution to Apollo 13's issues might seem impossible to us. But it wasn't impossible to Ed because Ed had an objective, he knew how things worked up there, and he knew how to come up with potential solutions.

So let's get you those same things for story. The first thing on the agenda is to learn is what it is you're trying to accomplish. And it might not be what you think.

2

WHAT'S A STORY?

What's a story? A lot of times when I ask this question in my classes, I receive answers like "It's a tale about a character" or "It's a narrative with a beginning, middle, and end." Someone might say it needs rising tension. Someone else might quote E.M. Forrester and suggest, "The king died and then the queen died is a story. The king died, and then queen died of grief is a plot." At which point everyone blinks and gets a bit of the deer-in-the-headlights look.

None of those answers help, do they? That's because they're not hitting the target.

What's a story? Think about it for a second. Why do you plunk down cash for one? Why do you stay up, reading past midnight in the bathroom, sitting on the edge of the tub and getting a weird bum? Why do you go back to books again and again? Why do we consume them?

When I ask it this way, most folks quickly realize the definition is not about the form a story takes—scenes, beginnings, climaxes, paragraphs —it's about what it does.

And what do stories do?

The answer to this question unlocks everything that follows. Unfortunately, in my experience, it's the thing that so many beginning writers miss, which makes learning this craft almost impossible because if you don't know what you're trying to accomplish, how in the world are you ever going to get good at it?

So let's pull back the curtain. A story triggers in the reader a certain type of experience. We make readers curious, make 'em laugh, cry, wonder, hope, fear, and shout in triumph. We often describe stories by the emotions they make us feel: thriller, mystery, romance, adventure, inspiration, tear-jerker. In fact, when we talk about genre, it's simply a label for a certain type of experience the story generates.

What stories do—successful stories, great stories, stories people actually pay money for—is generate a certain type of emotional ride with certain types of experiences along the way. This is the first mystery. This is the grand key.

Why do some readers pay hundreds of dollars on the stories they read each year? Why do some readers spend a tithe of their time with books?

They do it to feel what stories make them *feel*.

What's a story? It's the ride you take your readers on.

You must never lose sight of this. It's your goal. It's how you figure out what to look for in the stories you experience. It's how you figure out what you need to learn. It's how you judge whether something is working or not.

Many new writers don't know this and soon find themselves in a swamp of writing rules, rigid story structures, and a hundred other how-tos that have very little effect on the goal. Keep your eye on the goal. Your job is to continually improve your understanding of the experience you need to give the reader and how that's accomplished. Nothing else matters.

YOUR PERSONAL GENRE

Saying stories generate emotion is good, but it's too general. Because we don't generate suspense the same way we do surprise. And the methods used for those two experiences are different from the ones used to generate a feeling of attraction and romance. We need to know the specific things we want to elicit in our readers because until we do, it's going to be mighty hard to figure out how to do it.

Now somebody at this point might be getting concerned that this sounds mechanical. Like we're simply pushing people's buttons.

Let me put your mind at ease. Developing and writing a successful story is never a mechanical process. You yourself have to feel it. But we're not talking about how we develop the story yet. We're just talking about what it needs to do. The goal.

And you need to get specific. You need to discover the chief emotions people go to stories for. Except that's not quite right. What you need to identify are the chief emotions *you* go to stories for. Because you need to write what you love. Not necessarily what I love. You are your first audience. And there are a lot of different types of story experiences out there.

It's like the food we eat. Can you imagine anyone claiming that there's only one cuisine that all restaurants should serve—spaghetti and mashed potatoes? There's nothing wrong with that fare, but we'd laugh at the thought that it's the only food that can be enjoyed. One of the wonderful things about all the various foods is the massive variety of experiences they can offer. There's something for everyone. Well, the same goes for story.

ENJOYMENTS AND VICARIOUS THRILLS

Another way to look at this is to think of the vicarious thrills, excitement, or enjoyments we go to stories to experience. For example, you might enjoy the thrill of:

- Falling in love and having that love returned.
- A manhunt.
- A perilous adventure.
- Befriending a rare creature.

Or you might enjoy the satisfaction and enjoyment of:

- Doing something meaningful for a poor community.
- Finding redemption in the eyes of those you love.
- Succeeding at a high-powered job.
- Restoring affection to your marriage.

- Finding the lost cave in the Rocky Mountains that a mountain man wrote about in the 1700s that supposedly contains the remains of Vikings.

Think about the vicarious thrills you love and want to offer.

A METHOD TO IDENTIFY YOUR JUICE

The best method I know of to help you figure out the types of experiences that draw you is as follows.

1. Start by listing out ten of your favorite stories. They don't have to be the ten most favorite. Just ten out of the hundreds you love. They can be fiction, history, or biography. They can be novels, movies, or poems. This is a novel writing academy, so try to use novels. But don't feel you must. Just list some favorite stories.

2. Next, jot down the genre of each.

3. Then jot down what you liked about each story. What jazzed you? Think about the characters, setting, the main situation, and the way the whole thing unfolded, developed, and finished. Was there something about the beginning, middle, or end you liked? Did you love being transported to some exotic or wonderful place? Was there something awesome about the characters?

4. Don't jot down what you think you *should* like. Jot down what you actually do like. This should be fun. This is *your* list. If you like fancy prose, great. If you don't notice the prose much and don't care, great. If you like cliffhangers at the end of chapters, great. If you don't, that's fine too. If your big thing is stories about ponies, awesome! Your job is to accurately list all of the things that sparked *your* interest and turned *you* on.

5. When you've done this for ten of your favorite stories, look at what you've written and identify the things that appear more than once. 6. Next, mark the things you enjoyed the most.

If you feel ambitious, repeat the process with another ten stories.

7. Now, do one more thing. Write out anything you wish these stories provided more of but don't. For example, I have a friend who loves romances, but wanted ones that didn't focus so much on sex. She

wanted more sweet or "clean" romance. I have another friend who loves fantasy, but wanted more action and fun. I myself love thrillers, but don't like spending so much of the time with gruesome, serial-killing nut jobs. Instead, I wanted more humor and a focus on characters who had heart. <u>Whatever it is that you feel is missing or you want more of than you're getting, write that down.</u>

When you finish, you should see a pattern of delights. <u>This is your personal pattern. These are *your* draws. Focus on them. Be on the watch for when you feel them. As you do, you'll become more sensitized to them. And that will help you see what the storyteller is doing that generates them in you</u>. In the academy you'll learn how many effects work. But there's more insight to be had than we can teach you in the course. The good news is that because you now know what you're looking for, you can begin to discover what makes them tick.

Your draws might change as you start looking at stories this way. They may change as you grow older and other things become important to you. That's not a problem, <u>just as long as you know the delights and the hallmarks of the experience you want to deliver</u>.

A LIST TO HELP YOU START TO SEE

Sometimes new writers haven't thought much about the delights in stories and find it helpful to see examples of what I'm talking about. What I offer below is in no way exhaustive. And it's especially not what every author "should" love. In fact, some of the things listed below are mutually exclusive. I simply offer these to help you start distinguishing what it is you love about your favorite stories.

(A.) SETTING

With setting, <u>we're talking about the time period and location</u>. Examples include things like:

- The American Wild West
- Among the Amish in the 1940s
- Among the hippies in the 1970s

- Ancient Rome
- New York City in the early 1700s
- A future dystopia in Boise, Idaho
- An exotic place like Tahiti in the early 1900s
- Medieval Europe
- Modern-day India
- Modern-day small town in Britain
- The US frontier in the 1840 pioneer era
- The Persian frontier in the 100s
- The future in 2100 in Mexico
- The future in 2100 on Mars
- The sea during the reign of the Chinese pirate queen in the late 1700s
- Tolkien-like, Medieval fantasy world
- Victorian England
- Wild places like remote mountain region or desert today
- World War 2

Do you gravitate toward stories set in the past, present, or future? If it's in the past, is it during a certain period? Do you find yourself pulled to stories set in small towns, big cities, the frontier, the sea, certain countries, etc.?

SITUATION

The types of issues and opportunities the heroes and heroines of your stories deal with. Examples include things like:

- Adventure
- Aliens
- Black ops
- Combat
- Coming-of-age at a boarding school
- Court rooms
- Creepy horror
- Crimes of all sorts

Create Story Ideas that Beg to be Written

- Espionage
- Families
- Following your dreams
- Glitzy high-society stuff
- High school issues
- Horses and ponies
- Hospital emergency rooms
- Learning how to be a soldier
- Learning how to be a wizard
- Magic
- Manhunt or womanhunt
- Moral dilemmas
- Murder mysteries
- Mythical creatures
- Old folks coming back to kick butt
- Overcoming some huge hardship
- Pirates
- Political intrigue and threats
- Redemption
- Romance
- Space battles
- Slavery
- Sports
- Stopping bad guys
- Strange occurrence mysteries
- Technology gone wrong
- Teen dating
- War

Remember, this list isn't anywhere close to be exhaustive. I'm just trying to help you see examples of what I'm talking about.

 CHARACTERS

You might see a pattern with the types of characters you enjoy. They could be:

- Admirable
- Animals
- Attractive
- Big, fun characters
- Blue-collar
- British
- Cowboys
- Female
- Funny
- Gritty
- High-society
- Kids
- Male
- Not what you'd expect in the role
- Over-the-top people
- Peasants
- Physically strong
- Quirky
- Regular Janes and Joes
- Royalty
- Scottish men
- Sherlock Holmes smart
- Skilled in swords
- Soldiers
- Special agents or operators
- Spies
- Teens
- Tough
- Underdogs
- Wise-cracking
- Witty

Again, this list is not exhaustive. Look at the people you love in your books. See if the same types of folks pop up again and again.

COMPLEXITY

You might also prefer <u>a certain level of complexity</u> such as:

- Single point of view versus multiple points of view
- A few characters versus a massive cast
- Single storyline versus tons of storylines
- Shorter stories versus longer, sprawling stories
- A moderate learning curve (new names and jargon) or tons of new information and a steep learning curve

EXPERIENCE IN GENERAL

<u>Think as well about the experience in general.</u> Do you enjoy things like:

- A good cry
- A tear-jerker
- Action
- Behind the scenes insights into larger-than-life jobs, situations, processes, or places
- Big spectacle
- Bittersweet endings
- Can't stop turning pages
- Chapter cliffhangers or teases
- Character arcs where they come to new insights
- Discovering a character's cool backstory
- Double-crosses
- Fast, bam, bam, bam chapters
- Fun
- Happy endings
- Heart-warming endings
- Humor
- Immersion in the setting
- Inspirational moments
- Lots of character banter
- Lots of relationship dilemmas

- Mind-blowing surprises
- More dialogue than action and description
- Mystery
- Oh man, that would be so cool! stuff
- Poignant moments
- Scare the soup of out of you
- Slower chapters
- Snatching victory from jaws of defeat
- Something you'd like to be, do, or enjoy
- Tender moments
- Thought-provoking situations
- Thrilling action
- Tragedy
- Uplifting endings
- Wonder

Remember: these lists above are not all-inclusive. Their purpose is to get you thinking. Also, you don't need to write a book on your personal genre. Just take a half hour or so and jot down what you see. You will probably come back to your list a number of times as you learn to distinguish what it is you really love and what you dislike.

F. BRING OUT THE PIZZA

At this point you should have an enlightening list of delights. But you aren't writing for just yourself. You're writing for an audience, and the genre you choose promises your readers certain types of experiences. When you promise your readers a certain type of experience, you need to provide that type of experience.

If you fail to do that, you're going to have some frustrated customers. It's like going to a pizza joint and ordering a pizza. You smell the great pizza smells. You salivate, imagining the great pizza taste. The waiter brings out salad and root beer. You wait some more and finally realize that your pizza goodness is not coming. When you ask the waiter, he says, "Sorry, we decided you needed fried asparagus instead."

How are you going to feel? That's how your readers will feel if you don't give them what you promised.

So before you finish your list of effects, you need to identify what types of experiences readers are coming to your genre for. And you probably want to identify which are nice-to-haves and which are mandatory.

For example, if you're writing romance, one thing romance readers want is happily-ever-after endings. That's part of what they're coming to the romance book to experience. If you fail to provide it, you've failed to bring out the pizza. Romance readers also want a heroine they can identify with and a hero with whom they can fall in love. If you fail to provide those, you've failed to bring out the pizza.

Action stories promise to let the reader experience chases, escapes, fights, etc. If you don't bring out some fun action stunts, you've failed to bring out the pizza. Action stories also promise rug pulls. They also promise not to take you through long passages of navel-gazing.

Cozy mysteries have particular experiences that readers of cozy mysteries want. So do epic fantasies, space operas, scary stories, historical fiction stories, buddy stories, military stories, westerns, etc. So your final step is to identify the genre you're working in and what experiences are the must-haves.

Don't skip this step. You don't want to get to the end of your novel, publish it, and only then realize you promised a pizza and brought out squid. If you promised a pizza, bring out a pizza.

IDENTIFYING THE MUST-HAVES

How do you identify the must-haves? Let me suggest this process.

First, make sure you've read seven to ten novels in the genre that have sold well and readers seem to love.

Second, perform a quick analysis.

- Step back and list out their delights, just like you did for your personal genre.
- Identify what the books have in common.

- Think about books in the genre you didn't like and identify the reasons.

Third, go talk to a handful of other readers who enjoy the genre. Ask about their favorite books and what they enjoy the most about them. Then ask about those they disliked and the reasons.

At this point, you should have a good idea about the main experiences readers go to the genre for. You should have a feel for the pacing, the size of chapters, the types of endings, etc. But notice I didn't say you'd have an encyclopedic knowledge of them.

You don't need to do a 100-book research project. You don't need to do a 20,000 person survey. You don't need to read every bestseller in the genre for the last ten years. What you need is a good idea. Enough to get started. Because your goal is to write stories, not earn a PhD in literary analysis. As you continue to write and read, you'll refine your understanding. But you don't need an exhaustive understanding to begin. You'll learn as you go.

One last point. Some of the bestselling books may have things in them that you don't like. If you don't like it, don't include it. What you're offering is the same, but different. Bring out *your* style of pizza.

Once you've finished identifying the type of experience you want to deliver, it's time to figure out how to put it all together in a way that actually creates something that can be written as a story. And a big part of that revolves around what we talk about in the next chapter.

3
TRIGGER AND DELAY

We authors want this.

Bob simply must read one more page

We want to write books that people can't put down. We want kids to forget to eat because they're so engrossed in the story. We want adults to refuse to go to bed because they keep telling themselves, oh, just one more chapter. We want people reading in the car, at lunch, and, yes, we want people so engrossed they read our books in the tub and shower. And we want to be able to produce this effect reliably, on purpose instead of on accident.

The problem is that we're not always sure what generates that response. What makes a reader beg for one more page?

A few years ago I submitted a manuscript to my publisher, and they were taking their time getting back to me. But I had an idea for a story that had been percolating for a while, and I decided to write that story while I was waiting.

I wanted it to move like a freight train. It was an action thriller, after all, and I wanted the reader to find it mighty hard to put down. More importantly, I thought I'd discovered what would do that. At least part of it.

I knew I needed a likable, interesting character. I knew I needed an interesting situation. And something at stake. I knew my character needed to set a concrete goal to gain or retain whatever it was that was at stake. I knew my prose needed to transport the reader to the events. I knew there were specific effects that readers were coming to the genre to enjoy, and I had to deliver them. I knew all of that. But there was this other fundamental piece that was critical. If the book didn't have it, the rest of these things wouldn't matter.

And so I made sure to use it throughout the book. And then I released it.

What happened? I sold tens of thousands of copies of that book and got hundreds of positive reviews. And, wouldn't you know it, there's a theme running through those reviews. Here are a few of them. See if you can spot it.

- I picked up this book for a little light reading over Christmas break and couldn't put it down." –Live Great
- "My gosh what a story. I was on the edge of my seat the whole book and exhausted by the time it was over. Absolutely loved it even though I need a nap now." —Judy Glover
- "Couldn't put it down and almost read straight thru" —Mona Talbot
- "I could not put it down." —Alan J Anderson
- "Very well written fast moving and hard to put down" —Amazon Customer

Create Story Ideas that Beg to be Written

- "Riveting I did not put it down until finished" —Amazon Customer
- "It was very difficult to put the book down." —Amazon customer
- "You'd best find a comfortable chair when you start because you won't get up until you're finished." —Seven Shinall
- "I read in two days because couldn't put it down" —Olga Platt
- "I could hardly wait to go to the next page." —Edie English
- "Damn you John Brown. The last half of this book was so good that I stayed up until midnight last night to finish it when I had to be up at 0400 this morning" —Ian M.
- "I had trouble putting it down." —Amazon Customer
- "This truly is a book that I couldn't put down (much to my wife's displeasure)" —Dwight Diedricht

I share all that to show you my test worked. So what was I doing?

Well, it's the same thing television shows do to make sure you want to stay with them through the commercial breaks (usually two in a 30-minute show and four for one that lasts a full hour). It's what news programs do to make sure you tune in and stay with them.

- "House in West Valley burns. But the residents were saved by an unexpected hero. Details at five."
- "There's some weird weather coming. Mark will explain it all and why you need to be prepared tonight at ten."
- "Suppliers are recalling the spinach at thousands of stores. Tune in at five to see how to keep your family safe."

It's what all those goofy internet ads do that you find yourself clicking despite your better judgment.

For example, there was the time I went to a webpage to watch a video of the U.S. ambassador warning Syria. The big heading read, "Nikki Haley Warns Syria: U.S. Is Locked and Loaded."

Did I watch it? Heck no. Who cared about imminent war? My attention was drawn to the sidebar with an aerial image of some military hangar and the text below it which read, "MYSTERIOUS DESERT PROJECT. Forget Mars: The City of Tomorrow Will be in Arizona."

Mysterious Mars project out in Arizona?! Click.

Or there was the time I finished reading an article on a webpage, and it was time to get back to work, but down at the bottom was an image of the actor Gene Wilder in a black shirt and black cowboy hat. The headline below the image read,

"Most iconic line Of All Time, But He Was Never Meant to Say It In the First Place."

What? What was he never meant to say?!

And there was the image next to it of silver metal being poured into a small dirt mount with the headline "After This Man Poured Metal Inside An Ant Nest, What He Dug Up Was Magical."

An ant nest? By golly, what did he dig up?

Do you see what they're doing?

Do you recognize what I've been doing to you since the beginning of this chapter?

All of these examples use something I call trigger and delay. And it's one of the main things that engrosses readers in our story. What we do is trigger a desire in the reader and then delay the fulfillment of that desire. And the three main desires we trigger are:

1. Hopes and fears for the character.
2. Anticipation for something dramatic that's going to occur
3. A desire to know the answer to some question, puzzle, secret, or mystery

Please note that what we're triggering is in the reader, not necessarily the character. For example, the character might be a little girl on a swing in the park without a care in the world. But the reader knows about the woman standing in the bushes who's thinking she can sell that little girl for a few thousand dollars.

We as readers fear for the girl. We don't know what *will* happen, but we know what *might* happen and feel tension about those possibilities. However, the character is oblivious.

Always remember that trigger and delay is focused on the reader. If the trigger doesn't happen in the reader, it's not a trigger. It's a dud.

Trigger and delay is a huge part of keeping people engrossed in your story. When you learn how to do it, you will increase your readers' enjoyment.

In fact, these reader desires play such a central part in the story experience that building and releasing them determines, in a large part, story structure, including how we start our story ride, what we do in the middle, and how we end it. It affects how we begin and end chapters. It can even affect how we relay information in paragraphs and, sometimes, individual sentences.

So how's it done?

Well, we'll begin exploring that topic in the next chapter.

4

THE STORY SETUP

Hey, you turned the page. Gee, I wonder if that had anything to do with the fact that I triggered a desire in you and then delayed fulfilling it. Hmm.

Well, wait no longer. We can use trigger and then delay across:

- Books
- Chapters
- Pages
- Paragraphs
- Sentences

You'll learn about using it at the lower levels in the courses on developing your outline and writing chapters. Right now we want to focus on what's required to trigger the reader's attention for a whole book. Remember, you're trying to trigger these things in the reader:

1. Hopes and fears for the character
2. Anticipation for something dramatic that's going to occur
3. A desire to know the answer to some question, puzzle, secret, or mystery

A cracking good story idea, one that will trigger those things, requires five critical elements. Until you have all five, you'll struggle to plot. You'll write a few scenes and run out of gas. You'll feel like the story just isn't going anywhere. And that's because it isn't. It can't. A story isn't a story without all five elements. However, once you fill in the slots for these five things, your story will suddenly roar to life. Here they are:

1. Genre
2. Compelling character
3. THOM (Threat, Hardship, Opportunity, Mystery)
4. Goal to gain or retain something specific
5. Formidable obstacle

Later we'll add these elements:

- Interesting cast
- Cool locations

Those first five elements make up our story engine. If you want to take your readers on a ride, put these five elements together, and your car's engine will roar. Leave one or more out, and you'll pop the hood only to find your engine has been replaced by a raggedy, wheel-running gerbil.

Filling in the blanks on these elements is what creates story ideas that beg to be written. It does that because these elements trigger the three things we talked about in the last chapter. Yes, there are a lot of other delights we offer in our stories. But these are core. And because of that, the story setup will influence the structure of your whole story. Let's get a brief introduction to each of the five elements.

① GENRE

You already know a bunch about this. The genre is a label for a certain set of experiences. And we need it in the story setup because it tells us the types of THOMs, goals, and obstacles we'll need.

For example, let's say the idea of writing a story set in World War 2 Europe takes hold of you. If I tell you you're going to write a romance in that setting, you're going to think of all sorts of different scenes, characters, situations, and complications than if I tell you you're going to write about a mission where our characters need to go behind enemy lines to steal the German attack plans.

Deciding on the genre sends you down one path of ideas. It immediately tells you (and the reader) what kinds of awesome things they can anticipate experiencing.

2. COMPELLING CHARACTER

We love interesting characters. We want to watch them. We want to follow them around and see what they do. We also love to root for them and against those who oppose them.

Sometimes we can write a story with such a compelling situation (THOM, goal, and obstacle) that it overshadows the main character and makes them less important to the experience. But if we can create someone interesting, it heightens the desire to see what happens. If we can create someone likable, readers will start to care about what happens to them and begin to root for them.

3. THOM

Genre, setting, and a character aren't enough. Without a THOM there's nothing for the character to do and nothing really for us to care about. THOM stands for:

1. **T**hreat
2. **H**ardship
3. **O**pportunity
4. **M**ystery
5. Relationship

When the THOM shows up, the story starts because the THOM introduces the story's main question, which revolves around something bad the character wants to escape, something good he wants to experience, or some mystery he wants to solve.

A **threat** puts something important in danger. It might be a threat to our life, family, or friends. It could be a threat to our vision, our government, our job, or some beautiful location. There are all sorts of things we care about that might be put in jeopardy. Introduce a threat, and suddenly our character needs to take action.

A threat is something bad that might happen in the future. A **hardship** is something bad that's happening right now. We lose our job, or live in the cupboard under the stairs with a dreadful family, or are starving, or are slaves.

An **opportunity** is something awesome that we might be able to enjoy. Romance stories are all stories about a certain type of opportunity—the possibility of love that unexpectedly walks into the character's life. But there are more. There's the opportunity to get a great job, learn cool magic, become a spy, find a sunken treasure, and others.

Notice that the first three THOMs all revolve around some aspect of happiness.

Mystery is a little different. This piques our curiosity and makes us want to know the answer about some secret, question, or puzzle. There are murder mysteries, government secret mysteries, mysterious characters, and secret character backgrounds. There are stories about weird things going on like green lights coming out of the sewer that we can't explain. Or maybe, when we plow our field, we unearth some odd artifact that doesn't look like it's from Earth.

Please note that we don't need to introduce a situation that includes all four types of THOMs. Some situations include a combination. But it's not necessary. What is necessary is to make sure the THOM puts something important at stake. Something important the character stands to lose or something wonderful she stands to gain.

For example, if a character's house plant is stolen, that's not as compelling as when a character's little sister is stolen. A house plant is not so important. A little sister is. Unless the house plant links the character to a murder, or is the last one of its kind in the world and can give the person super powers.

In addition to making sure the THOM puts something significant at stake, we also want to make sure the issue resonates with our target readers. While there is some overlap, middle grade readers are probably not going to be interested in some things adults are and vice versa. Historical romance readers are probably not going to be interested in the same THOMs readers of historical military fiction are.

The key thing to remember is that the THOM introduces the main issue that's at stake in the story. Until it appears, you're just warming up your engines.

4. GOAL TO GAIN OR RETAIN SOMETHING SPECIFIC

When the THOM is introduced into the character's life and puts something large enough at stake, the character will naturally want to do something about it. He or she is going to want to gain or retain the thing at stake—whatever it is that will make them secure, happy, or give their life meaning. For example, if someone is trying to kidnap the character's daughter, he'll want to retain that good thing in his life. If the character is struggling financially, she'll want to gain a new job and financial independence. And if we like the character, we're going to root that she gets it.

Because our brains are wired for concrete facts, the goal will generate more juice in the reader if it's specific. For example, let's say the character's sister is kidnapped. We don't want to make the goal something general like "obtain family security." Nobody cares about something abstract like that. It sounds like the gobbledygook you'd see in a business presentation. Our brains live in specifics. And the specific goal here is to get Julie back from those three cowboys.

Furthermore, when we have a specific goal, the character can begin to formulate a specific plan, a specific how, for reaching the goal. We as readers can then worry about whether the obstacles and opposing forces will thwart the character.

Finally, when you have a clear goal, you can flip it into a yes-no story question. Having a story question that can be answered with a yes or no simplifies and clarifies. And that clarity will do wonders with helping you keep the story straight in your mind. The question for the story

38

above is "Will Bill, the father, save Julie?" If Julie is able to act on her own behalf, and you want to give her some scenes, then her story question is "Will Julie escape?"

5. FORMIDABLE OBSTACLE

When reading stories we don't want to know what will happen. We want to know what *might* happen and worry about the possibilities.

Why? Because hoping and fearing for something we care about rivets us. Mystery rivets us. So does anticipation. And all of those require uncertainty.

Think about sports. What games are the most thrilling?

It's not the games where you know you're going to obliterate the other team. The most thrilling games are when our team's the underdog, and there is a possibility we might win, but there's a larger possibility that we won't. And as the game progresses, we get ahead, then fall behind, and we go back and forth between the fear that we'll lose and the hope that, oh my holy heck, we might win! There will be a moment when all seems lost, and then a moment when things turn, and we just need one more touchdown or basket or goal to win, but time is running out, and the odds are long, and there's no way we can see how we'll make it. And then the quarterback makes one last valiant attempt and throws a hail-Mary pass or the team runs a trick play, and suddenly, with one second left, we score. We score and snatch the victory from certain defeat!

Those are the games that bring people to their feet and make them cheer. Those are the games that make our hearts palpitate and give us a rush of joy. And it's all because there was uncertainty in the outcome. And there was uncertainty because formidable obstacles stood in the way of our success.

ROXIE

So the setup consists of the genre, character, THOM, goal, and a formidable obstacle to that goal.

Later, we're going to spend a chapter exploring each of the story setup elements in detail. For right now, let's just see some examples of how this story setup works. To do that we're going to use Roxie.

Back in 2016 I came across this picture in an ad.

Roxie Hurlburt, Co-owner, Mercer's Dairy

Roxie's name, face, and the fact that she ran this dairy were immediately compelling to me. Now, you might not think she's compelling at all. That's fine. We aren't all zinged by the same things. The point is that I found something I thought was cool. But did I have a story?

No, of course not. I need five things to have a story. And so I started generating ideas for each element until I had five that crackled with electricity.

Let's look at some examples of <u>what happens when you know (1) what you're trying to achieve (cool ideas for all five elements), (2) how stories work, and (3) some techniques for generating potential solutions until you find some that start to sing.</u>

EXAMPLE 1: GRANDMA KICK-BUTT

How about this one?

1. **<u>Genre.</u>** Action thriller
2. **<u>Compelling character.</u>** Female, Roxie, sixties, gun-toting, tractor-driving, horse-riding, tough-as-nails widow rancher. Loves spending time with her little ten-year-old, cow-girl granddaughter.

Create Story Ideas that Beg to be Written

3. **THOM**. Threat. Roxie's making pies with her granddaughter, hears a ruckus, looks out the kitchen window, and sees her neighbor's dog mauling yet another one of her calves. After chasing the dog off, she's had enough. She gets in her old truck and goes over to demand that her neighbor pay her for the calf and put the dog down. But instead of confronting the neighbor, she interrupts a drug dealer and his goons murdering the neighbor as punishment. The bad guys (maybe there's a woman with them) see her and come after her. Roxie rushes to her truck, and the granddaughter pops up from backseat, having snuck in to surprise her.
4. **Gain\Retain**. Life, security. She wants to escape these thugs. She wants to get her granddaughter to safety.
5. **Formidable obstacle**. Roxie doesn't have her phone, or she doesn't have service out in this rural area. She's in an old pickup. They're in a new SUV and another fast car. They have lots of guns, and she left hers at home.

Are you feeling some interest in this story? Is it begging to be told? It's begging me. However, it might not be begging you. If not, that's okay. I want to write the stories that beg me to write them. You want to write the stories that beg you.

The point of the example is to see how the elements work together. And one of the neat things about knowing what the elements are is that you can immediately begin to play around with them, sketching different options, until you land on five things that crackle with electricity.

SETUP BRIEF

I like working and developing in the format shown above. It's loose and free and lets me generate lots of options for the story setup elements. However, after I've come up with the idea, if I want to summarize it so I can communicate it in a brief description, I sometimes put it in the template below I call the brief. You might find the template helpful as well.

However, I want to caution you. The goal is not to create this summary of the story setup. The summary format doesn't have any special power. It's just a way to condense things. Having said that, here's the template.

BRIEF STORY SETUP SUMMARY TEMPLATE

1. In this [genre]
2. [Character] is an [adjectives] [vocation] working for [hope or dream]
3. When [inciting incident / THOM occurs].
4. Will she be able to [gain/retain specific thing]
5. When she must [struggle against formidable obstacle]?

To use it, you just fill in the blanks. So that Grandma Kick-Butt story above might come out like this.

1. In this action thriller
2. Roxie is a mid-sixties, gun-toting, tractor-driving, horse-riding, tough-as-nails widow rancher who loves spending time with her 10-year-old, cow-girl granddaughter.
3. When Roxie interrupts a drug cartel killing, the bad guys come after her.
4. Will she be able to get her granddaughter to safety
5. When she is outmanned, outgunned, cut off in the middle of nowhere, and more of the cartel roadblocks her exit?

Did you notice how the story question simplifies and clarifies the whole matter? You don't have to create a brief, but making the effort to put the setup in this format can help a great deal. If you decide not to create a brief, I do recommend at least taking the character's goal and formulating the question the story will focus on.

EXAMPLE 2: GRANDMA FRAME JOB

Let's try some other options.

Create Story Ideas that Beg to be Written

1. **Genre.** Mystery.
2. **Compelling character.** Female, Roxie, sixties, smart, put together, but starting to forget things, manages the ice cream co-op so she can earn enough to help pay for her daughter's cancer treatments.
3. **THOM.** Mystery and threat. She loses a deposit for $30,000. Then an investigation shows something is not right with books. A younger woman at the co-op who has always thought Roxie needed to go wants her job and is campaigning to get her out. Roxie is accused of negligence, then criminal fraud.
4. **Gain\Retain.** Find the lost money. Prove innocence. Stay out of jail so she can help her daughter.
5. **Formidable obstacle.** Roxie's been cut off from the files and the co-op. The cops and the younger gal are building a case. Roxie suspects the money was stolen, and someone is trying to frame her, but there are no leads. And the only one that believes her is romantic old Ernie, who she grew up with.

And here it is in brief:

1. In this crime mystery
2. Roxie is a mid-sixties, wise-cracking manager of an ice cream co-op who is working to help pay for her granddaughter's cancer treatments
3. She's starting to forget things and when she loses a deposit for $30,000 an investigation shows something not right with books. A younger gal at the co-op accuses her of negligence, then fraud.
4. Will Roxie be able to find the lost money, prove her innocence, and stay out of jail so she can help her daughter
5. When the cops are building a case, she's been cut off from the company, and the only person to help her is romantic old Ernie?

Ideas that beg to be written are not made up of one story idea. They're made up by a bunch of them. And coming up with ideas for these five elements is critical.

EXAMPLE 3: GRANDMA SMUGGLER IN SPACE

Let's do it again, this time in space.

1. **Genre.** Science fiction action.
2. **Compelling character.** Female, Roxie, sixties, smuggles on planet. Earning to help pay for granddaughter's chance at being a space explorer.
3. **THOM.** Mystery and threat. A deadly, enforcer robot chases her down, and Roxie is given a choice—take something to the good ranching people she was smuggling to that will kill them or watch her granddaughter be recycled into fertilizer.
4. **Gain\Retain.** Happiness for her granddaughter and good people Roxie has been helping.
5. **Formidable obstacle.** The robot goes with Roxie, and she discovers it wasn't sent by a criminal organization, but some shadowy part of the government, one that nobody messes with.

Here it is in brief.

1. In this tale of science fiction action
2. Roxie is a mid-sixties, mechanical wiz who is smuggling to help pay for granddaughter's shot at being a space explorer.
3. When she makes a risky run, she's chased down by a deadly, enforcer robot and given a choice—smuggle in something that will kill innocent people or your granddaughter will be recycled.
4. Will Roxie be able to save the people and her granddaughter
5. When the robot is sent with her, her granddaughter is taken, and Roxie discovers she's can't go to the cops because this is

being orchestrated by one of the most dangerous parts of the government?

Are you anticipating being on the edge of your seat, hoping Roxie beats these guys? Are you wanting to urge her on? I'm thinking Roxie has some criminal smuggling connections who might help. And I'm rooting for her to take out the nasty robot and the dirt bag government folks and get her granddaughter back!

EXAMPLE 4: GRANDMA MONSTER SLAYER

A compelling character like Roxie can play all sorts of roles. Here she is in a heroic fantasy.

1. **Genre.** Heroic fantasy.
2. **Compelling character.** Female, Roxie, sixties, bawdy. She washed out of mage training when she was young, but knows some small magics. She lost all of her family but her teenage grandson to war a decade back. She lives in a village and just wants to see her grandson and the kids there grow.
3. **THOM.** Threat. People begin vanishing from the vale. And then they find evidence a korog (an ancient monster) is dragging them away.
4. **Gain\Retain.** Safety. Protect the children and her grandson.
5. **Formidable obstacle.** Korogs are dark, shadowy, and powerful. And when the village sends their strongest trio of men to go outside for help, the korog kills them all. Roxie and the others are trapped in the vale, and all that's left is a motley crew of teens, older folks, kids, and regular moms who don't know how to fight.

And here it is in brief.

1. In this heroic fantasy
2. Roxie is a mid-sixties, bawdy, village grandmother who wants

nothing more than to see her teenage grandson grow up to be a good man.
3. However, when people of the vale begin to vanish, she discovers a korog, an ancient monster, has taken up residence in the woods and is behind the killings.
4. Will she be able to save the villagers and her grandson
5. When the three strongest village men are slain, she and the others are trapped in the vale, and there's nobody left who knows how to fight. It's just a ragtag collection of ordinary women, teens, kids, and older folks.

As you were reading, <u>did you get any cool ideas?</u> Anything you think would <u>make Roxie or the situation more fun or interesting?</u> Was there <u>a way to up the stakes</u>? Or <u>increase the obstacles</u>? Or <u>put a twist in here somewhere</u>? If not, <u>by simply asking these types of questions, your miracle brain will start to come up with options</u>.

EXAMPLE 5: GRANDMA TRAILER PARK

Let's do one more.

1. **Genre.** Urban fantasy, like the X-files.
2. **Compelling character.** Female, Roxie, sixties, trailer park grandma who used to ride with a motorcycle gang. She's just trying to live in peace and raise her granddaughter to be a good woman who hopefully avoids some of the mistakes grandma made.
3. **THOM.** Mystery and threat. People in the trailer park are being attacked by shadows. Roxie's granddaughter reports she sees dark beings before the attacks. And then the dark creatures begin to stalk her granddaughter.
4. **Gain\Retain.** Safety. Find out what the creatures are and eliminate their threat to protect her granddaughter.
5. **Formidable obstacle.** Roxie has no idea what's going on or who might help. Doctors diagnose her granddaughter seeing

these beings as a mental illness. And then the Department of Family Services threatens to take her granddaughter away.

Here it is in brief.

1. In this urban fantasy
2. Roxie is a mid-sixties, ex-biker, trailer-park grandma who is trying to raise her granddaughter.
3. When people in the trailer park start to be attacked in the shadows, Roxie's granddaughter reports seeing dark beings. And then the creatures begin to hunt her granddaughter.
4. Will Roxie be able to protect her granddaughter
5. When Roxie has no idea what's going on, doctors diagnose her granddaughter with a mental illness, and then the Department of Family Services threatens to take the child away?

If I begin to think about who else might be there, I can see Roxie interacting with various trailer park characters. A romantic guy with a booze problem that can sing and play like Elvis. A younger construction worker who just lost his wife and is trying to rebuild. And older woman with a shotgun. I can see Roxie maybe reaching out to a few of the members of her old biking gang. I can see her maybe talking to some beaded, hippy-dippy, occult specialist.

A story setup that gives you the "oh, man that's cool" or "gee, that would be fun" or "yes, that's perfect!" feeling is the kind of setup you're looking for. It's the kind of setup that will spark other ideas when you ask additional development questions like who else is there and what's the setting like.

But it doesn't always start out that way. If you don't feel the zing at the beginning, don't despair. That's actually normal. All you need to do is continue to sketch options for the five elements until you start to feel that electricity.

Now, we could have used Roxie in other stories. We could have developed a romance, a buddy story, a story about her running for office, one about her going back to school, or forgiving her estranged husband, or taking back what some pirates stole from her, and dozens more. <u>The key thing to see here are the five elements. That's your development goal.</u> When you have them, they will enable you to reach your ultimate goal of triggering interest.

The question now is <u>how do you come up with an interesting character, compelling THOM, and formidable obstacle in the first place?</u> It's one thing to be able to identify and describe these elements. It's quite another thing to come up with them from scratch. What are the super-secret techniques authors use to generate terrific ideas?

We're going to talk about that in the next chapter.

5

SIX PRINCIPLES THAT WILL UNLEASH YOUR CREATIVITY

Remember that list of three things you must learn to write killer stories? Number three was knowing effective methods for generating options for elements of the story until we find ones that achieve our purpose.

It sounds easy enough, but I can't tell you how many new writers I've talked to over the years who are stymied in their efforts because they don't know how to do this. <u>Not knowing the principles of creativity is an author slayer</u>.

It almost slew me. Five years after that award and first publication, I was participating in a week-long writer's boot camp taught by Orson Scott Card. It was my last hope. I'd stumbled around unable to finish anything for five years. And I hoped this boot camp would give me whatever vitamin I was missing. The first four days of the boot camp did give me tons of insights *about* story, but not about how to produce one. And by Thursday evening, I'd failed to finish my story for the class. We were supposed to have turned it in on Wednesday, and I was out of time. Oh, <u>I had lots of interesting bits about setting and character. But I could not put it together into a story</u>.

That Thursday night, I was sitting at a table at a restaurant, poking at the chicken and mashed potatoes on my plate and staring at the awful truth—I simply didn't have what it takes. I'd flown out to this boot camp and used the money I could have taken my family to Disney World with, chasing this stupid dream.

On the bright side, which didn't feel so bright at the time, I told myself that at least now I could give writing up and save myself further torment. I would finish a lifeless, going-through-the-motions story for the boot camp, turn it in, politely listen to the reports of everyone's experiences, and then I'd give my writing books away, toss all my manuscripts in the garbage, and never look back. Because it's true you can walk away from writing and be happy.

I sighed, looked at the clock, and figured I had enough time to give it one more try. An idea came to me. I didn't have much hope, but what could I lose? I gave my idea a shot, and suddenly the lights turned on, the music started playing, and the story rolled out in front of me like a carpet.

There they were: the beginning, middle, end. I saw scenes in bam, bam, bam fashion. I scribbled a few quick notes on my paper, then hustled for the exit. John Brown had a story to write! As I rushed out, I saw another boot camper waiting in line. He looked over, and I waved my paper in the air with excitement. "I've got it! I've got it!" And then I ran out into the parking lot.

I sped to the hotel and wrote furiously that night. I got up early and wrote the next morning before class. I wrote during lunch, during our breaks, and all Friday evening. I turned my story in Saturday morning to the other boot campers. Some of them groaned. It was 7,000 words. They'd already read eighteen other stories. But after reading it, most came back with smiles on their faces, and the reports of their experience showed it was a huge success with them and Card himself. After the boot camp, I sent the story out, and it sold, then sold reprint rights, then sold audio rights. It was even included in a best-of-the-year anthology.

So what happened? One minute I had the wrong DNA. The other I had a barn burner in my hands. What was the difference?

Well, it wasn't me. It wasn't a change in DNA or personality. And it definitely wasn't a brushed velvet jacket. It was a couple of principles of creativity. That's all that was holding me back. <u>I was minutes away from giving up because I lacked a fundamental knowledge of the principles</u>

and techniques of generating ideas. Luckily, I recognized what I'd been missing. Afterwards, I dove into the principles and associated techniques, and I'm going to share them here.

You need to know these principles because an incorrect understanding of creativity will hogtie you and toss you off the cliff. Let's avoid that. In this chapter, I'm going to give you the principles. In the class, you'll use them to generate tons of ideas.

PRINCIPLE 1: FEED YOUR BEAST

Your imagination is like a beast. Feed it, and it will get up and roar. Starve it, and it will lie around like a dust mop and gather flies.

You must feed your imagination. This is the first principle of creativity.

Some of us might feel we don't have much of anything we can use for food. Most of us are not Ann Franks, CIA agents, or little old ladies caught in terrorist plots. But we don't have to be. Because idea food is all around us. We just need to go gather it. We just need to go hunting. And what we're hunting is zing.

Zing is any idea that turns you on, sparks your imagination, or stokes your desire. Zing tingles your cool meter. "Dude," "Yes," "Ah," "Oh baby," "Man-o-man," "Great oogily boogily"—these are all common responses when you come across these types of ideas.

Most zings are small tingles. Sometimes they're zaps. And every once in a while you'll get a freaking gigawatt monster that shakes you about and leave you breathless. These ideas are out there all over the place, available for the picking. Your job as a writer is to go get them and bring them back for others to enjoy.

One summer I taught a teen writers workshop where we met one day each week for three weeks. During the first class I introduced the concept of zing and told the students they were to hunt for 10 zings each day.

They were dismayed. They groaned. Ten! Was that even possible?

The next week all of the students came back bubbling about all the things they'd found. One of them said it had changed her outlook on life: her world, which had been relatively humdrum was suddenly filled with the cool. The other students agreed.

We all are limited by what we can perceive and focus on. Our working memories are so small it's easy to focus on the many mundane business-of-life things and miss the wonderful show of delights that goes on around us.

This is what hunting for zing does for you. It quite literally changes your world because you start seeing it through a different lens.

So how do you do this? Where do you go to find lots of good eats?

Deploy Your Dragnet

This first place to look is where you already are. Your normal day-to-day activities. All you have to do is be on the lookout. All you have to do is turn your zing sensors on. It's like deploying a drag net—it catches whatever it comes across.

Just be on the lookout. And when something cool comes along, capture it. Use scratch paper, the back of a receipt, a notebook, a manila folder file, a camera, a sketchbook—whatever. Just capture it when it comes. Create a file and put it in it.

Many of the ideas will just sit in the file. That's fine. The principle here is that you're looking. You're sensitizing yourself. And you're getting better and better at noticing things and thinking about how they might be used for character, THOM, obstacle, plot twists, etc. The more you do it, the better you'll get at finding more.

The other neat thing is that these little scraps and snippets have a way of combining at the oddest moments, and suddenly you have more than an itty-bitty old zing, you have a freaking power plant! Another benefit of the dragnet is that you get ideas you'd never in a million years come up with on your own.

For example, I happened to see a book while browsing a section in the library. It was about how to raise chickens in your apartment.

What? Chickens in your apartment?

Zing.

Because I make it a practice to hunt zing, I stopped and started to read. I captured the ideas and jotted down some ways to use them in a story. What if my character's neighbor did that? What if his kooky sister did? Maybe his wife decides they need to be more self-sufficient. Or maybe she's told a neighbor she'd take care of her chickens. Wait a minute, chickens in the apartment, could I use that in a murder mystery?

On another occasion, I was reading an article about ancient history and learned about a girl that was sold to cover her father's debts.

How dreadful. How dramatic.

Zing.

I captured it. Could that happen today? How would that work? What if it was someone else who kidnapped a girl to pay off debts? Hey, could I use that as a THOM for my current book?

On another occasion, I was reading an online newspaper that was sent to me each week and came across an article with this:

> "The monkey, which costs $15,000, is what Truelove envisions as the ultimate SWAT reconnaissance tool. Since 1979, capuchin monkeys have been trained to be companions for people who are quadriplegics by performing daily tasks, such as serving food, opening and closing doors, turning lights on and off, retrieving objects and brushing hair. Truelove hopes the same training could prepare a monkey for special-ops intelligence."

A SWAT monkey?!

Zing. Zing. Zing.

Could this primate be put to nefarious purposes? What if he stole something incredibly valuable? What if a major thief uses them? What if it was used in war? Or espionage? Or what about a monkey used in a plot to kill the president?

On another occasion, I was talking to a friend, and he told me about another one of his acquaintances who lets his toenails grow to horrible lengths. He said they look like claws. It was incredibly disgusting.

Zing.

A disgusting zing, but zing nevertheless. Could a minor character in my story have that quirk? What if it was someone who worked with the main character in the office? Or the main character's sidekick in a medieval army squad?

On another occasion, I read this:

"GARDEN GROVE (CBS) — An Albertson's supermarket on Harbor Boulevard was evacuated Monday after a burglary suspect fell through the ceiling to the ground near a cash register."

Through the ceiling? What the heck?
Zing.
What in the world was he doing up there? What if he was a good guy? What if he was undercover with some thieves? What if he'd been forced into some plot? And how high was the ceiling—did he swing down on some wiring?

On another occasion I stumbled across a picture of an article in the Duluth News Tribune on Saturday, June 8, 1907.

TWO MEN KIDNAP NUN FROM SCHOOL AT WEST END, OUTRUN MOB AND ESCAPE
   Abductors Boldly Enter Room Where Sister Borromea Is Teaching And Carry Her Away
PUPILS SPELLBOUND BY TERROR
   They stand mute while abductors drag shrieking woman to street and thrust her into hack, but recover in time to give chase—are joined by hundreds of people in the neighborhood, but the team is fast and outfoots them—no clue to where the outlaws have secreted their victim—relatives of the sister, who is the daughter of Edward Digle, formerly of Itasca, are suspected of being responsible for the desperate act.

Zing!
Why was she kidnapped? Was she working for a criminal gang? Was she a ransom? Did she have something they wanted?
Could I have ever come up with any of these on my own? Never. But now they're in my zing file, and I can pull them out at any time and feed them to my creative beast.
Make it a practice to capture food for your imagination.

Create Story Ideas that Beg to be Written

Ask Your Zing Questions

I want you to look at the list of zings above. Did you notice what I did after I captured each of them?

I asked questions.

What if this? Why that? What is going on? Could some form of this be used as a THOM, character, obstacle, or twist in a plot?

A lot of creativity is asking questions relevant to what you're trying to accomplish and then generating some answers. So when you come across zing, ask a few questions that relate to story elements. What if this was part of this or that THOM? Could I use this with a character? How might I use this for a plot turn? What could go terribly wrong?

Ask questions, and your miracle story-telling brain will start to come up with options.

Try Things

Sometimes you will be presented with an opportunity to experience something new. May I suggest you take it?

After moving up into the hinterlands of Utah, I one day saw this sign.

No, that's not a W

As a regular Joe, I might have said, um, tempting, but no, and driven on. As a zing hunter, well, this was not an opportunity you came across every day.

I went to the festival with my brother-in-law, and we stood in the line with our paper plates. They scooped up parts for us from one of the Dutch ovens with a generous helping of cooked onions. We went over and sat on the rodeo arena bleachers with our root beers, cut off chunks, looked at each other, and partook, trying not to think too much about what we had in our mouths, which was pretty much impossible.

No, they do not taste like chicken.

They do taste like something else many people find delicious. But I'll let you identify what that is on your own.

When you get a chance to try something new, try it. You'll get marvelous details, wonderful ideas, and inject occasional adventures into your life. If, nothing else, you might get lunch out of it.

Go Hunting

A dragnet is good, but you cannot rely on random catches to deliver all the ideas you need. This means you will need to also look for zing for a specific story requirement in territory outside of your own current experience. Find an idea for a story setup element to try it on for size.

Sometimes you have character and setting but no THOM. Sometimes you have a THOM but no character that has any life to them. Sometimes you have a character and THOM, but can't come up with a series of obstacles. In these cases, you don't want to wait for what might happen to swim into your dragnet. Instead, you want to go hunting.

The more THOMs you see, the more THOMs you'll be able to produce for your stories. The more characters and people you see, the more characters you can generate. The same goes for obstacles, surprises, rug-pulls, twists, lines of dialogue, beginnings, endings, and so on.

It works for the topics you write about as well. The more you know about crime, the better your crime ideas will be. The more you know about horses, the more options you'll see for your story featuring horses.

The more you know about drones, the more and cooler your options for your story about killer drones will be.

So where do you go looking? There are two territories I've found that are loaded with good zing eats.

Other Stories

I get an unlimited supply of ideas from other stories. Those stories can be from the news, history, friends, acquaintances, scripture, gossip, fairy tales, poems, movies, TV programs, summaries of actual court cases, novels, magazines, biographies, etc.

For example, let's say you need to find a THOM for your story but just can't come up with one. Go look at the THOMs in a dozen novels or TV programs in your same genre. If they don't spark ideas, look at a dozen more.

Let's say you need a character. Try scanning through a dozen articles in the news or look through a book about some colorful characters in history. Go out online and google to see the faces of those in your character's vocation. Sooner or later, you'll start getting ideas that start to crackle with electricity.

Research

I also get a huge number of ideas from plain old research. It helps me find unexpected, convincing details as well as THOMs, characters, and obstacles. The ground of research is thick with zing.

For example, in one of my Frank Shaw thrillers, I wanted to write about my ex-con character teamed up with a female sheriff. I decided I needed to get more information on what it was like being a female cop. So I read some books on it and learned a number of fantastic details. But, even better, an acquaintance of mine was a cop in the nearest big city. I asked him if he knew any female officers. He did: a female sergeant.

And so I contacted her and asked if she'd be willing to let me ask a few questions. She was happy to chat with me. And I so I interviewed her and got a ton of good insights, including details about female cops struggling with the body armor built for men and how they often have to use their social skills instead of brawn to deal with situations. And all that informed how I thought and wrote about my character.

The best way I've found to research is to start simple, and then go deep. So I start with juvenile books on a topic, Wikipedia articles, and documentaries. Then I move into thicker, more adult texts. If I can go do something or talk to someone who has done it, that's even better. Nothing like shooting guns to learn about shooting guns. Nothing like paragliding to get details about paragliding. Nothing like going to a location to get the local feel.

Research is one of the joys of writing. Be a hunter. Go out there and capture the zing.

PRINCIPLE 2: MONKEY SEE, MONKEY ADAPT

Nobody creates anything in a vacuum. That means everything is like something else in one or more ways. We are all writing what we do because of something written by others. We all see what other authors do and imitate and adapt it for our own use, even if we don't know we're doing it. So don't worry about being original and doing something nobody has done before because that isn't how creativity works.

Star Wars felt so original when it came out, unless you were steeped in Flash Gordon, Doc Smith, and others. If you were, it was just another variation of something that had already been done before.

Hunger Games. Wow! That was original. Except, it has elements of Shirley Jackson's "The Lottery" and reality TV.

Well, what about Shakespeare? Surely, he was an original. Um, no. *Othello, Romeo and Juliet, Hamlet*, and a dozen others—all variations or retellings of earlier works someone else had written. Shakespeare was a man who knew how to be "inspired" by his sources.

I just read a James Patterson novel called *Hunted*. It's now one of my favorite action thrillers of the last few years, and it's a retelling of "The Most Dangerous Game" transported to modern-day England.

James Dashner wrote the bestselling *Maze Runner* series, which was made into a series of movies, by adapting ideas from the TV show *Lost*.

Shall I go on?

Been done means squat.

Readers don't want something wholly different anyway. They want the same, but different. The same experience, but a little different.

That's why we have a gazillion romances published every year. That's why we have an unending parade of cop shows. It's why, every year, more epic fantasies are published. One J.R.R. Tolkien, one detective, one romance simply isn't enough. We want to take those rides over and over again.

Every year for the last eleven years, my wife and I have taught her classes of seventh and eighth graders how to develop stories. To date, they have produced more than six hundred variations of "The Three Little Pigs." They've made the pigs humans, they've made them zombies, they've made them rabbits. They've put their characters in ranching towns, amusement parks, and China. They've made the wolf a creepy doll, Mrs. Brown (their lovely teacher), or gangsters looking for money. Hundreds and hundreds of variations of "The Three Little Pigs," and they've all been different. And we'll have hundreds more before we're through. And those will be different as well.

We are monkeys. Or at least distant cousins to them. We build on each other's work. It doesn't matter if we're talking about making cars, baking cakes, or developing stories. Monkey see, monkey adapt. It's one of the reasons why we rule the planet.

If you don't have any ideas, go look at what other authors have done. It's a field packed full of zing. Find something you like and use it.

The Same, but Different

How do you do the same, but different? You take what they did and use different details. Or you put it to a different purpose.

- A similar character with a different THOM.
- A similar THOM with different characters.
- A similar THOM in a totally different location or time.
- Etc.

For example, *The Lion King* has the same general story situation as *Hamlet*, but it's set in Africa, with different animal characters instead of humans. *Hoodwinked* is the story of Red Riding Hood, except the villain is a cute sociopath bunny who wants to rule the baking world. *Pride and Prejudice and Zombies* is a parody of the classic romance.

Let's say you like the wry humor of a character in another story you love. Great, imitate that dry humor in yours. Let's say you love the villain-comes-back-after-you-kill-him climaxes. Great, write one for your book. Let's say you love Scottish men in time traveling in kilts who make heroines swoon. Wonderful, put the brothers or cousins of those laddies in your book. If you like the five-man band approach to casting, great. Create a five-man, five-woman, or five-kid band. If you like how some author opened his book, try it with your story.

Copyright

Nobody can copyright facts—real people, events, things, and places. If you want to set your story in London with Winston Churchill, do it. If you want your character to drive a Ford, have them drive the Ford.

Nobody can copyright a type of setting, character, obstacle, THOM, opening, conclusion, genre, plot, or plot element. They can't copyright a theme. They can't copyright a writing style. They can't even copyright the slang they come up with. So if you read a story where one character calls another character a "crow-pecked poop bag," well, you can use that in your book too.

Nobody can copyright ideas. For example, nobody can copyright the idea of robots, space ships, pirates, serial killers, wizards, etc. They can't copyright character types like gunslinging drifter, billionaire hero, army guy who chews cigars, granny with a shotgun, etc.

What we copyright are the specific sequences of words we use to tell our tales. And the specific expressions of the various types. So don't go copying paragraphs. Or the specific characters you find, unless they're real people.

For example, let's say you love Lee Child's fictional Jack Reacher character. If you put him in your books, using his name, description, background, habits, etc., you're probably going to get into trouble because you're copying the exact expression of the tough-guy drifter type. But if you put a character in your books called John Puller and

Create Story Ideas that Beg to be Written

make him similar to Jack Reacher in many ways, you're fine, as David Baldacci demonstrates with his best-selling John Puller series.

If you love the robot R2D2 from Star Wars and copy it into your story, you're begging for a lawsuit. But if you put in another small robot that is similar to R2D2 in some ways, you'll be okay because nobody can copyright the idea of small robots. Or even robots with three legs that talk in bleep bloop.

<u>Find story elements that zing and adapt them for your purposes.</u> And if you have a question about whether you've gone too far, go read a book on copyright or talk to a copyright lawyer.

Go Wide

When looking for inspiration, you're looking for new twists or combinations of familiar ideas. <u>And a good place to look for new twists and combinations is outside your genre.</u> This means you want to <u>read widely.</u> <u>Read anything that catches your interest.</u> <u>Try things that aren't your usual cup of tea.</u> <u>Things you think you don't like.</u> <u>Things that might not seem to apply to your story.</u>

For example, back when I was a kid, I loved John Wayne. This was in the ancient days before DVR, DVDs, and VHS. It was back in the days where you scanned the TV schedule in this thing called a newspaper because if you missed your program, you missed it. Maybe forever. I loved the annual showing of John Wayne's movie *The Cowboys*. And when I saw it on the schedule, I'd circle it and count down the days. All of my friends at school would watch it. And the next day we'd talk about it and play games, imagining ourselves fighting bad cowboys.

Fast forward five hundred years. John Brown is wanting to write a new coming-of-age epic fantasy series. And wouldn't you know it, he thought about the story setup for *The Cowboys*. The story was totally outside the genre. And it was perfect. In it went with my twists and adaptations and details.

How many other John Wayne epic fantasy mixes are out there? I don't know of any. But even if they were all over the place, I wouldn't care. Because this combination of epic fantasy and John Wayne is particular to me. It's my baby, the same, but different.

Everything we humans create, including stories, builds on what has come before. Nothing we do is completely original. And that's one of our super powers. Don't eschew your super power. Use it, Spiderman. Use it!

PRINCIPLE 3: EXERCISE FARMER'S FAITH

The ranchers up here know something that a lot of city folks don't.

Every fall, the ranchers bring the cattle out of the hills and back to their fields. The cattle overwinter in those fields, and every day, the ranchers feed the cattle the hay they grew in the summer. In the spring, the ranchers move the cattle back up into the hills. And then they do something curious—they get into their tractors and drive up and down every inch of their fields, dragging a collection of old tires or bars and chains behind them.

Do you know why they do this?

It because the cattle have left behind a whole winter's worth of manure. And the farmers know that manure is gold. It helps their crops grow. What the ranchers are doing is breaking up and spreading the manure around.

Crap makes things grow. And that applies to story ideas just as much as it applies to farmers' fields.

Instead of rejecting our stupid ideas, we need to be like the ranchers and cherish them. "Hello there little piece of crap. I love you. I'm going to write you down, because I know you're going to make good things grow." When you write down your bad ideas, you free yourself from your internal critic. You also feed your beast and spark new ideas.

If instead of cherishing your crappy ideas, you recoil in horror, impatience, or frustration; if you immediately shoot your ideas down with some version of no, dumb, no, cliché, no, a rip-off, heck, that one doesn't even make any sense—no, no, no. If that's how you approach it, you will shut the creative part of your mind down. Trust me on this. When generating options, you need to be able to consider the weird, odd, dumb, dull, and crazy. If you do, you will fertilize your mind, and flowers will grow.

You're no different than the kids in my wife's middle school language arts classes. Every year, we help close to a hundred kids come up with all sorts of great ideas. Year after year, one of the keys to their success is making sure they exercise farmer's faith.

When a student gets stumped, I ask them for the dumbest idea they can think of. I ask them to give me dumb on purpose. Then give me dumb again. And again. When we combine farmer's faith with the other principles in this chapter, we never fail to help a student start generating ideas.

So you may begin with a crappy story setup. That's okay. "Hello there, crappy story setup. I'm going to cherish you by writing you down because I know good things will grow."

Hello there, crappy character...

Hello there, crappy story turn...

Hello there, crappy ending...

Exercise farmer's faith with your first draft because first drafts frequently have a lot of crap in them. Exercise farmer's faith when you run into a story snag and your first solutions are crap. Exercise farmer's faith when your beginning is dull. Exercise farmer's faith until you've finished your tale.

Be nice to the crappy things that come out of your brain. Because those crappy things lead you to other things. Crappy ideas are not a sign that you're not a writer. They're a sign that you're actually working through the creative process because crap is part of the process. Stamp that on your forehead: crap is part of the process. So cherish your manure. Trust the process. And know that your dreck will produce flowers.

PRINCIPLE 4: SKETCH, THEN DRAFT

One thing that's helped me write more in less time is something I borrowed from visual artists.

Visual artists frequently make a number of sketches or thumbnail drawings before they paint. It saves tons of time. And it leads to a much better finished product. The reason for this is that sketches allow visual artists to quickly try a whole bunch of different options until they find one that sizzles.

It also frees up a visual artist's creativity because sketches exert zero pressure. You don't like one? Fine. It's just a sketch. Toss it and try another. You want to try something crazy, odd, or unusual? Fine. Sketch it and see where it takes you. You can try a dozen options quickly this way.

The same principle applies to writing. You don't have to write a whole novel to see if the character, story setup, or plot is going to work. You don't have to write a whole chapter to get an idea if the chapter is working. You don't have to write a scene to try out a story turn.

Instead, before you dive into the details, you can sketch a number of options, improving upon earlier sketches or trying something totally different. And when you land on one that carries some zing, you can then spend the time rendering that one in detail.

Just to be clear, I'm not talking about drawing. I'm talking about writing down a rough idea for a character, scene, story setup, etc. You can use sentences, a quick bullet list, or paragraphs. The key is that it's just a sketch.

For example, it's always easier for me to write a scene if I sketch what it's about beforehand. I then might sketch how I expect the scene to flow. All this sketching doesn't take more than three minutes. And the crazy thing is that this approach usually takes less time than if I just dove in.

You can sketch the flow of a whole novel in a single page. Or you can do it in three, five, ten, or twenty pages. The point is that it's a sketch that allows you to consider an idea, riff on it, or toss it.

You can sketch multiple options for a character in just a few minutes. You can sketch multiple options for an ending in the same amount of time.

You can also sketch by writing a tentative draft of a chapter or scene. The key word here is tentative. So you jot down a few lines about what the scene should be about, then begin to render it in detail. You might finish the scene in one take and feel it's fantastic as is. Or you might finish it, knowing there are lines of dialogue or narrative that don't quite sparkle like you want them to. You might also get into the scene, start well, then run out of gas or into a snag.

It's no big deal. This isn't the final draft. It's a tentative draft. This means you can stop, step back, and try to figure out what the issue is. If you need to you, you can try it again with another take of the chapter. Some of my chapters require one take. Others require more. I had one chapter that required twenty-four takes until I finally nailed it. And when I finished it, I copied that take over to my book document which contains the finals of all the other chapters.

Sketch, then draft. This is one way you exercise farmer's faith. You might be tempted to jump right into the detail work, but a little bit of sketching up front, a little exploration of options in this quick form, will save you time and unleash your creativity.

PRINCIPLE 5: SPEND ENOUGH TIME TO KEEP YOUR OVEN HOT

We all know that before you can bake anything, you've got to get the oven to the temperature that will produce all the desired chemical reactions. We all know it takes time to get the oven hot, and so one of the first things we do when baking is turn the oven on and get it warming up.

Now, imagine letting the oven heat for one minute, turning it off, then coming back again a few days or weeks later, turning it on for a few minutes, then turning it off and leaving again. Imagine doing that over and over.

Will you ever be able to bake anything in that oven? No. It's not because the oven is faulty. The oven is perfectly fine. It's because you didn't give the oven enough time to get hot. And once it got hot, you didn't keep it there.

Your mind works the same way. It needs time to get hot. If you write for an hour or three one week, then put aside your story and come back a few weeks later, work on it a bit, then put it aside and come back a few weeks later, you will be forever warming your oven up, and you won't produce anything.

It's not that your mind is faulty. It's not that you aren't creative. It's that you're spending all your time warming up. Specifically, you're spending all your time bringing the story up in working memory, trying to remember where you were, what elements you need, and what the dang thing is about.

If you want to be productive, you need to let your mind get hot by putting in consistent time on the project. I find that if I spend anything less than seven hours a week on a project, my production falls completely apart. Seven barely keeps me in the game. If I can spend ten, twelve, fifteen, twenty hours a week, my creativity and production shoots through the roof. The ideas are better, they come faster, and I can write with speed.

Please note this doesn't mean you have to write in two- or four-hour blocks.

You can get quite a bit done in a twenty- or twenty-five-minute writing sprint. A sprint means you focus exclusively on the writing—no social media, texting, etc. Anybody can focus for twenty minutes. If you have more time, take a five- or ten-minute break then do another sprint. You can even squeeze this down to a ten- or fifteen-minute sprint where you generate options for some story problem you're working on or write some action or dialogue. You'll be surprised how much you can get done in twenty minutes if you focus.

You can also talk through things aloud with yourself while doing something else. For example, you can talk aloud to yourself and generate options while driving somewhere. If you need to, pull over and jot your ideas down. You can talk to yourself on your daily walks. I take two sheets of paper that I've stapled together and a pencil and talk through things aloud as I go. You can talk things through while washing the dishes. You can do it while mowing the lawn.

You can also find times where you're just sitting around. For example, if you need to pick your kids up from school, instead of messing around with texting or some game, you can take your laptop and do a twenty-minute sprint while waiting.

If you can get big blocks of time, great. If not, breaking your writing up this way allows you to perhaps get a sprint or three in the morning before the day begins. It gives you some time during the commute, more time during your breaks, and then even more time in another sprint or three after work.

However you do it, schedule in the time needed to get and keep your oven hot.

PRINCIPLE 6: FOLLOW THE RULE OF COOL

A few years ago, Larry Correia and I decided to pitch a presentation at a large, local writing convention. We figured we'd teach the attendees some principles of creating a science fiction action plot. The convention liked the idea and booked us.

Now I'd run such sessions before. Larry and I had, in fact, done some of them together. However, I knew if we ran them like we had before, we'd start at the beginning of the story development and never get to the plot. With audience participation, an hour simply isn't enough time. I suggested we start the session with a good sketch of the story setup already in place. That way we could then help the audience see how to figure out what comes next.

Larry agreed and we set a date to develop it. When the day came, I drove to Larry's house and sat with him in his living room. Larry's son Joe sat on the stairs going down to the basement, listening in. At the time he was around eleven.

After some initial chat, I said, "Okay, let's get started. What do we want—space opera, dystopia, *Blade Runner*."

Larry said, "Hey, Joe. What's cool?"

Joe popped up from his spot on the stairs and said without hesitation, "Giant robots, bandits, and murderers."

Larry and I looked at each other. Dang, that *was* cool. And so we ran with it. Forty minutes later we had a sketch of the story setup for a great novel. And that's what we used in the interactive presentation at the convention. But the story doesn't end there.

A few years later, Larry called me up. He said Baen Books was wanting him to maybe do some collaborations. Among others, he immediately thought of our story idea. He pitched it to Toni Weisskopf, his editor. She said she loved it. And so Larry and I began a collaboration.

And it all started from the question "What's cool?"

We're in the entertainment business. That means people come to our stories looking for a terrific experience that may include thrills, poignancy, inspiration, laughs, suspense, wish-fulfillment, insights, etc. And that all starts with asking what's cool. Of course, following the rule of cool has some implications.

Your Zing, Not Mine

First, let's remember what we said about zing. Good ideas carry current, they spark your interest, they tug your heart strings, and turn you on. A good idea is like an electric jolt. Sometimes it's very small; sometimes it's overpowering. It's the feeling of "cool," "whoa," or "oh, boy, this has possibilities."

But notice I said they spark *your* interest.

You're not looking for what turns me on. Or your friend. Or your writing hero or mentor. You're looking for what turns *you* on.

The only way you can judge whether an idea is good is by *feeling* it. It must spark you. And what sparks your imagination might not spark mine.

That's okay. Forget me and the others. Follow your zing. Follow what jazzes you.

Try to Figure Out How It Can Make Sense

Second, sometimes, after thinking about a cool idea for a moment, you might realize it doesn't make any sense because things wouldn't work that way, or your character wouldn't do that, or it's anachronistic, or a hundred other reasons.

You might be tempted to toss it. Don't. You'll write best when your mind is crackling with electricity. If it's cool, first try to figure out a way for it to make sense.

For example, in that novel Larry and I worked on together, we wanted to use mech suits. However, mech suits didn't make sense from what we knew of combat. Why dress up in a ten- or fifteen-foot suit? Why not just send out killer robots? And who is going to be standing up vertically and making themselves a big, old, fat splendid target anyway?

But we didn't toss out the idea. Mech suits were cool. In what situation would mech suits make sense? We put our minds to work on that question, and, wouldn't you know it, our miracle monkey brains started looking for answers.

What if the terrain was hilly woods and robots couldn't maneuver well there?

What if there was some electronic signature the robots made that drove the local kaiju nuts?

What if...

We figured out something that made sense to us, and we kept our cool mech suits in the story.

If it's cool, use it. If it doesn't make sense, try to figure out a way to make it work. If you can't, at that point set it aside to be used in another story. But if your idea is cool and doesn't create any big logic gaps that will throw you or your readers out of the story, use it. Because it's cool.

Ignore the So-called Writing Rules

A third implication is that something cool might break one of the hundreds of so-called writing rules that wander about and bully unsuspecting authors.

I remember being on a podcast where we discussed one of these rules. Immediately after that podcast I recalled a book by a best-selling author that was full of exactly what we had just pontificated upon. More importantly, I'd loved that novel. As had thousands upon thousands of others.

Suddenly I realized we on the podcast had gone at the topic all wrong. The measure is not whether our writing conforms to a bunch of arbitrary rules. It's whether it's interesting.

There are so many arcane writing rules out there. Well, to heck with them! Most of them are garbage anyway, having no connection to the reader experience. The only thing we should care about is whether our story is interesting. Nothing else matters.

Find Those with Your Same Tastes

The final implication of following the rule of cool is that you can't please everybody. So don't try. What's cool to you might not be cool to me. That's okay. There's no book that's loved by all, or even most, readers. Please read what Thomas McCormack, who spent twenty-eight years as the CEO and Editorial Director of St. Martin's Press, said about this.

"An author needs a lot more than one person to succumb to his literarily seductive charms, but, like Saul, he must realize that he doesn't have to—and indeed cannot—capture the hearts of every possible reader out there. No matter who the writer, his ideal intended audience is only a small fraction of all the living readers. Name the most widely read authors you can think of—Shakespeare, Austen, and Dickens to Robert Waller, Stephen King, and JK Rowling—and the immense majority of book-buyers out there actively decline to read them." (*The Fiction Editor, The Novel, and the Novelist*, p8)

Dwight V. Swain captured the same idea and suggests what we should do about it.

"The thing Character wants, the danger that threatens fulfillment of this desire, and the decision he makes, determine what specific readers will enjoy the story. One likes sex and violence, another tenderness and love, another the competitive striving for success, another intellectual stimulation. Relatively few college professors are Tarzan fans–and even fewer sharecroppers succumb to *Finnegans Wake*. The trick, for the writer, is merely to pinpoint audience taste…then to refrain from attempting to inflect his copy on the wrong people." (*Techniques of the Selling Writer*, p137)

The best advice is to write the kind of story you want to read. Then go find those with the same tastes and share it with them.

Have Fun!

Please note that you'll run into snags and story problems when developing and writing your stories. All writers do. And those moments can be frustrating. However, if you're always a droopy dog or wringing your hands when developing and writing your story, then something with your approach might be a bit off.

Writing stories is about going out and finding all sorts of cool stuff and then bringing it back to share with the reader. When we're doing it right, some of the time should be full of fun and adventure. If we're writing sad stuff, well, maybe fun isn't the right word. Maybe poignant is better.

The point is that we're developing an experience we love. So find a way to enjoy the ride. Follow the rule of cool.

YOU NOW HAVE THE BASICS

If you recall, the key to story creativity is knowing these three things:

1. The experience you want to deliver
2. How that experience is produced
3. Principles and methods for generating ways to get you there

You've identified the effects you're trying to create in the reader. You've learned how the story setup generates the core effects. And you've learned six powerful principles for coming up with potential solutions.

It's now time to put these principles to work and start to develop the story setups for a number of stories. To help you with that, in the next few chapters I will dive into more detail about each of the story setup elements so you can see more clearly how things work and what you're trying to develop potential solutions for.

6

COMPELLING CHARACTERS

Readers don't want to know what will happen. They want to know what might happen, and then for 90% of the novel they want to worry about, puzzle over, and anticipate the possibilities. At that point, after all that trouble, readers want the character to pull victory out of the jaws of defeat so they can exhale a big sigh of relief...until the next book in the series.

To begin that ride, you need to trigger in the reader the following things:

1. Hopes and fears for the character
2. Anticipation for something dramatic that's going to occur
3. A desire to know the answer to some question, puzzle, secret, or mystery

Presenting a compelling character with a significant THOM is one of the main ways to trigger that response.

However, our readers won't hope and fear for just anyone. Some people who are in terrible trouble evoke only pity or antipathy. Others generate so much dislike that we actively root against them. We need a

THOM, but clearly that's not the only thing that's required. So what else must we have?

WHAT MAKES READERS ROOT FOR A CHARACTER

Readers will only hope and fear for someone they think is deserving or pursuing a deserving cause. All of us have an automatic scale of justice inside of us. We can't turn it off. Nor can we ignore it. It's very simple. If someone's bad outweighs their good, then we think they deserve bad outcomes. Conversely, if someone's good outweighs their bad, we think they should receive good outcomes.

A boy breaks his arm and he whines, whines, whines about it all day long. He makes all his friends listen to him talk about how hard it is, going on and on and on. He tells his teachers he can't do his school work because of it. He mopes at home in front of the TV, then steals his sister's money to buy candy because he has this awful injury and he deserves a treat.

Are you going to root for this kid? Probably not.

Another boy has a broken arm. But this one doesn't whine. In fact, when his dad falls ill, the boy goes out and with his one good arm mucks out the horse stalls. And this despite terrible pain. He does this because his dad was going to lose his job if he didn't. Then the boy comes back in and cleans himself up and doesn't say a word about it.

Do you like that second boy? Do you want good things for him?

Of course you do.

Problems aren't enough. They're only half the equation. For us to root for someone, we have to feel they're deserving. Or if you like the term better, you can say they need to be likable.

So what makes someone deserving or likable?

That's going to be slightly different for each person because our moral codes are all slightly different. If you feel it's a sin to kill animals, you might feel conflicted reading a story about a rancher who needs to get his cattle to slaughter. If you feel unions do nothing but harm, you might not enjoy a book about a union boss trying to force a corporation into compliance. Nevertheless, there are many virtues and vices that people hold in common. Usually, we feel people are deserving if they have more of the positive traits listed below.

Positive Traits

- Kind
- Stands up for little guy
- Funny
- Sacrifices for someone else
- Good-humored, doesn't take himself too seriously
- Courageous
- Hard-working
- Actively tries to fix her own problems
- Hopeful

Negative Traits

- Cruel
- Bullies others
- Dull
- Selfish
- Whining
- Cowardly
- Takes himself too seriously
- Sanctimonious and self-righteous
- Lazy, only wants to snivel or groan about her problems
- Sad sacks

We feel people that tip the scales toward the positive traits deserve good things and those that tip it the other way deserve bad ones.

A big part of our appraisal of the situation depends on the person's motive. We look at both the act and the reason why they did it. For example, let's go back to that example of the kid with the broken arm that mucked out the horse stall. We'll love him if he made that sacrifice out of selflessness. We'll feel something different if he does it only because it allows him to hide his and his father's crime (maybe they killed someone and have temporarily stashed the body in the barn under the muck in a stall).

If we want our readers to root for our characters, then the character's cause needs to fall on the noble side of the equation. This doesn't mean the characters themselves have to be paragons of virtue. Deservingness is weighed on a scale. Just as long as the characters tip the scales the right way, we will feel they're deserving. On the other hand, if they cross the line the other way, we'll turn against them.

For example, let's say your lead character is a thief who steals money from retired folks. That's bad. In most situations we wouldn't like her. But in your story she's trying to save a kid from being kidnapped and sold into the sex slave trade. In this instance, our character may be a thief, but the justice she seeks outweighs the harm she causes, and we're going to root for her.

Now let's make our lead a child molester. He's trying to capture a brutal drug cartel murderer who has just escaped prison. Along the way he has his way with a few children.

Who are you rooting for this time?

Not the child-molesting scumbag. We hope the drug cartel guy finds the child molester and offs him. Or at least roughs him up and leaves him tied up on the front steps of the local police.

So you don't have to have perfect people as your leads. In fact, it's sometimes more interesting to have someone with foibles just like the rest of us. But when those foibles turn into things we find despicable, we'll turn against those characters.

And vice versa. For those of you who have read or watched *Pride and Prejudice*, did you notice how you rooted against Mr. Darcy when we interpreted his actions as smug condescension? The moment he changed, and we learned of it, we cheered for him. It was all a matter of deservingness.

If we want to hope and fear for our characters, they need troubles. But the characters also need to weigh in on the deserving side of our scale of justice. When they do, they become admirable, likable, heroic.

In fact, heroes, the ones that make us stand up and cheer, are those people that put their own happiness at risk to do the right thing for someone else. They're the very embodiment of deservingness.

But we're not done yet. We might have characters who are completely deserving, but they are so boring we can't muster any interest in them.

WHAT MAKES A CHARACTER INTERESTING

One of the chief joys of stories is meeting new and interesting people and getting to spend time watching them work through the interesting situation the THOM creates.

Except I shouldn't say people. While related to us, characters are not the same species. James N. Frey captured this in *How to Write a Damn Good Novel*.

> "Characters are to a novelist what lumber is to a carpenter and what bricks are to a bricklayer. Characters are the *stuff* out of which a novel is constructed.
>
> Fictional characters—*homo fictus*—are not, however, identical to flesh-and-blood human beings—*homo sapiens*. One reason for this is that reader wish to read about the exceptional rather than the mundane. Readers demand that *homo fictus* be more handsome or ugly, ruthless or noble, vengeful or forgiving, brave or cowardly, and so on, than real people are…Even if he is plain, dull, and boring, he'll be more extraordinary in his plainness, dullness, and boringness than his real-life counterparts."

A key to making *homo fictus* interesting is to exaggerate something about them. You may try exaggerating any physical, social, mental, vocational, or emotional ability, trait, or type. Below I list some of the things I think have the biggest draws. Please note that your characters don't have to exhibit all of the traits listed. The traits here are simply options to get you thinking. Follow your zing when choosing which ones to use for a given character.

Fighters

We are immediately attracted to folks who take the bull by the horns and fight for their dreams and what's right. These folks are scrappy and show courage in the face of danger. They are determined to overcome any obstacle that comes their way. We like characters who are confident and bold. Characters with attitude.

Resourcefulness

We are interested in folks who can overcome difficult, even impossible, problems by being clever and resourceful. If their gun breaks, they attack with a flower pot. If they're barred from entering a place, they disguise themselves as the toilet lady and get in. If the villain takes them prisoner, they figure out how to escape with a paperclip. These resourceful people might bend the rules a little bit or a lot, but they don't give up. The find creative, sometimes mind-blowing, solutions to solve their problems.

Special Power, Skills, or Abilities

People who have power draw our interest. That power may be one of many varieties. They may be super rich and drive the coolest cars and have the most luxurious houses and clothing.

They might have a position of power like the CEO of a big company, the general of an army, or the leader of some gang. But it doesn't have to be huge. A single cop draws attention. As does an IRS agent on your doorstep. The foreman of a crew has some power. The character might not even be the one to hold the reins of power but be a spouse or counselor of someone else who does.

They might have physical strength. They may be fast or strong or just huge individuals. They might be super athletic and can scale cliffs or swim in a raging sea. Maybe they have been trained to use deadly weapons or be one themselves.

People with extraordinary skills or talents draw our interest as well. In fact, ability is a type of power. And just like those with the other types of power, these folks evoke wonder, respect, and sometimes awe. We are fascinated by those who can do things well or have some gift.

Maybe they have an exaggerated ability for selling, making money, framing a house, painting, doing gymnastics, reading, hacking into computers, skydiving, firing weapons, riding horses, hunting, stalking prey, getting people to like them, cooking, or a thousand other things. Maybe, like Edna Mode in *The Incredibles*, they have the ability to design amazing super-hero outfits.

We are interested in folks who are really good at what they do for a living. They're not just detectives, they're Sherlocks or Columbos. They're not just soldiers, they're top marksmen. They're not just businessmen, they're moguls.

Give your character an ability or two. Make them good at what they do. It might help them solve the problem in the end, it might not. Either way, because they're *homo fictus*, you want to exaggerate their power, abilities, and skills.

A Larger-than-life Situation, Vocation, or Past

Another thing that makes characters interesting revolves around the character's circumstances. Maybe the character is normal guy in an extraordinary situation. He's a plumber caught in a murder plot.

Or maybe the character's vocation is larger-than-life. She's a CIA officer, smuggler, or a spy. Maybe he raises wolves or is a bounty hunter. Or hunts bears with a pack of dogs and a horse.

Or maybe she had an extraordinary job or experience in her past and fought in a war, survived a plane crash and two-hundred mile journey in the wilderness, starred in the movies, worked for the president of the United States, participated in a man hunt, or was at one time an outlaw.

Wish-fulfillment

We cannot help but be interested in characters who are, do, or have things we want, characters who are in situations we find attractive. In fact, this is one of the main draws of fiction–experiencing something wonderful or cool, even if it's vicariously.

What's one of the reasons why James Bond and other action heroes are so popular? Among other things, it's because so many of us would love to live the adventures those heroes do. We would love to be the type of guy who knows how to fight like a super agent and gets to use all the high-tech gizmos and drive the deluxe cars.

Create Story Ideas that Beg to be Written

How many young adult stories are about characters finding fairies or dragons or aliens? How much of fantasy is about having the powers magic grants? Wouldn't it be cool! Of course it would. That's wish-fulfillment.

How many stories feature folks who are rich? When we read, we get to step into that world. More wish-fulfillment.

How many stories feature characters caught up in events that seem more important than the events in our lives? <u>It's exciting. We get to step into that world and feel that excitement. And that's wish-fulfillment</u>.

We can see the same thing in romances. Phyllis Pianka states it this way in *How to Write Romances*:

> "You cannot write an engrossing romance novel until you create a heroine the reader wants to identify with and a hero the reader can fall in love with . . . they are idealized; the heroine is someone women would like to emulate: nicer, prettier, thinner, more intelligent, though not necessarily all of those things. She will have a flaw but it will be a minor one . . . the hero is the ideal lover and husband and father . . . Above all, he must be the man with whom every woman would like to fall in love."

Whether it's romances, thrillers, mysteries, or some other genre, we love it when a story provides us a bit of wish-fulfillment.

You can take a moderate approach, or you can exaggerate it. So not only is the guy rich, he's a billionaire. Not only is she strong, she can take down the biggest male fighter in the bar.

As with anything, what's desirable to you might not be what's desirable to me. Maybe I'm interested in anyone who has served in the armed forces or lives with some kind of risk and adventure. Maybe you can't stand that and are enthralled instead by horses. Maybe you'd like to fly airplanes, but I'd love to fly dragons. One guy is drawn to those with happy marriages full of laughter. Another is drawn to the freedom of single life. You write your stories, and I'll write mine. But we can both <u>make our characters more interesting to us and our natural audiences by adding, when it fits, some attractive fantasy.</u>

Good Looks

A character who is good looking attracts us. It may be the eyes, hair, hands, build, or way they stand. In visual media like movies, we see their attractiveness and automatically respond. In text, we have to help the reader imagine by focusing on certain things. If we want to convey sexuality, we draw attention to certain parts of the body. If we want to help readers imagine handsomeness and beauty, we draw attention to the face, smile, jaw, hair, etc. and other things that convey strength or elegance and grace.

Quirks

We are often drawn to characters that are eccentric, odd, or have some exaggerated quirk. Maybe he's a loud-talker, a mumbler, a guy who takes his three parrots with him where ever he goes. Maybe he's super thin. Or a cab driver with glasses so thick his passengers immediately wonder if they'll arrive alive. Maybe she has squeaky shoes. Or always smells of lemons. Or attracts bees with some special perfume because she says their buzzing is better than yoga. Maybe she's one of those people that walks around in their sleep or holds loud conversations with ghosts. Quirks are wonderful tools to make secondary characters more interesting.

Humor

We love to laugh. And so anytime you can create a character that does this to the audience, they will be interested in them. It might be our characters use dry sarcasm or witty one-liners. Or maybe they're one of those humorous types like the logical smart one; the lovable loser; the neurotic; the dumb one; or the one in his own universe. Or maybe you put the characters in humorous situations. Maybe the super-skilled hero has to deal with a belt buckle that won't work. Maybe instead of chasing the bad guys with a motorcycle, he has to use a bicycle. Whatever the type of humor, anything that makes us laugh or chuckle generates interest.

Surprise

We are intrigued by characters who play against type. The more unexpected, the more surprising it is. So maybe you have a plumber who quotes Shakespeare to his customers. Maybe you have a mixed martial arts fighter who is a mom with three kids. Maybe the hero is scared to death of dogs. Maybe the villain has a fear of spiders. Maybe the cutthroat millionaire business owner is a knitting granny. Maybe the bearded and tattooed biker carries around a book of scripture and reads it during quiet moments. Maybe the super spy loves yogurt. Anything that runs against type or is just plain unexpected for someone in that role or vocation will work. This includes the character's motives as well as appearance, mannerisms, hobbies, etc.

Danger

Anyone who poses a threat demands our interest. This is one of the reasons we pay attention to villains. Exaggerate the threat, and we pay more attention. Recall that many aspects of happiness can be threatened. It doesn't have to be a threat to life, limb, or property. For example, someone may threaten my relationship to my wife or my acceptance in a group or community. You can make good guys or bad guys more interesting by making them more dangerous.

Secrets

We love mysteries. And it's wonderful to give characters secrets. The bigger, the better. It might be the character's secrets present a bit of danger. Or hint at something dramatic. Maybe the character has a past life as a special agent they don't want to talk about. Or maybe they have a past they don't like to talk about because it might ruin what they're trying to do now, e.g. an ex-con trying to go straight and get a job. Either way, we love to wonder about them and then have our questions answered in surprising ways. And we love it when the reveals affect the story. For example, when what we learns turns a villain into a good guy. Or when what we learn amps up the suspense.

Fish Out of Water

When we move characters out of their element, it evokes anticipation for laughs and drama. A country cowboy in the city. A fussy neat-freak out camping. An accountant who knows nothing of combat is asked to become a soldier. The church lady who has to work with strippers. The more you exaggerate just how out of place the character is, the more fun you can have.

A Note

Most of the traits above could be used for bad guys as well as good guys. But don't make the mistake of thinking that making a character interesting will make them deserving or admirable. For example, humor can be given to characters we root against. Or maybe the character is mind-stealing beautiful, but uses that beauty for terrible purposes. Interest and sympathy for a character (or their cause) are different things.

HUMANIZING A CHARACTER

Sometimes we want to make a character more relatable.

One way to do this is have these folks deal with the normal orneriness of things and day-to-day issues the rest of us deal with. For example, the big agent's shoe has a hole in the sole that keeps letting pebbles in. The powerful king gains weight and can't mount his horse like he used to. The super detective gets shut out of a bed and breakfast because he didn't wipe up the water in the bathroom, and the owner is super finicky. The big-time business guy misses the garbage truck. The spy's gadget goes on the fritz.

Another way to humanize is to give the character a life outside the story that includes a non-plot goal or dream that's important to them. Maybe they love cooking and want to open a crazy burger joint. Maybe they mentor hard-luck kids. Maybe they want to do nothing more than spend time with a granddaughter or helping horses that have been traumatized.

A third way is to give them small flaws. So maybe the hero has a hard time controlling his temper. Or maybe he is afraid of flying. Or has a weakness for pink frosted cookies. Or can't do math.

HEROES

What traits must your heroes have?

As discussed above, we want someone to root for. For that to happen, the character must tip the moral scale to the positive side. The hero can be a good guy or a bit of a rogue, just as long as we agree with the cause he's engaged in. One of the most effective ways to do this is to have the hero be self-sacrificing for others.

You can add additional weight to the good side by building sympathy for him. You do that by giving the hero some hardship, threat, or wound in his personal life. For example, his new wife left him for a richer man; his dog died; his child was lost to drugs; his car is unreliable, and he doesn't have the cash to get it fixed; etc.

Second, the hero must be a fighter, determined to overcome all obstacles in her path. Otherwise, there is no plot. And nobody to cheer for.

Third, the hero needs to be clever and resourceful. Bozos don't win the day. Instead, they irritate and frustrate the readers. We want to hope for our characters, and there's not much you can hope for when your character is a blockhead.

Finally, the hero will be someone the reader is going to spend a lot of time with. You probably want that time to be enjoyable. That means your hero will need one or more of those other things that make characters interesting and enjoyable—things like power, abilities, larger-than-life past, quirks, against type traits, etc. Some genres require some of them. Others don't. Whichever ones you choose, follow the rule of cool and make your main characters colorful.

ANTAGONISTS AND VILLAINS

What about the bad guys? What do they need?

An antagonist is anyone who opposes the hero. A villain is a special type of antagonist who sends the morality meter crashing to the dark side. Villains have base motives like greed, hatred, lust, jealousy, etc. They are self-centered, cold-hearted, and merciless and couldn't give a flying flip about who they might hurt.

Whether you have a reasonable antagonist or a cold-hearted villain, the main role these folks play in the story is to generate anxiety and suspense in the reader. They do this by making us fear for our hero or his cause. There are other effects we can use antagonists for such as generating poignancy about the human situation by generating reader sympathy for them or making them a tragic character. You can see an example of this in Javert in *Les Misérables*. But such effects are secondary.

For an antagonist to make us worry the hero will fail, the villain must be a credible, significant, and immediate threat all the way through the book until he or she is defeated or wins. If the antagonist is not credible, the reader will see there is no real threat. If the threat is not significant, who cares? If it's not immediate, again, who cares?

So how do we make an antagonist like that? We make him or her smart, powerful, and dedicated to doing something we root against (because it's just plain wrong or because we love our hero and want the best for her). We make the antagonist appear seemingly unstoppable. That means he has the hero outgunned, outmanned, and is two or three steps ahead. We want the hero to be the underdog. That way we keep our reader worried that our hero might fail.

You can have all sorts of antagonists—liked by many or few, kooky or calculating, eccentric or plain, noble or sadistic—just as long as they remain significant, immediate, credible, and seemingly unstoppable threats. The minute they lose threat status, the game's over because at that point fear, anxiety, and suspense in the reader vanish.

So that's character theory. How do you sketch that to make it come alive in yours and the reader's mind?

7

THE CHARACTER SKETCH

A novel is something you read. It's not something you watch. It's not a movie. It's not TV.

Many folks gloss over that fact, but it has significant implications because you're not showing your readers the story.

You're not showing them characters.

You're not showing them anything.

Instead, you're helping them *imagine* characters, setting, and action. And the process for viewing something is neurologically different than imagining something from text. This has significant implications for how your build your characters. Let's first understand the process, then how that affects what you develop.

IMAGINING, NOT VIEWING

When we look at something, we can take in huge amounts of information all at once. When we read, we can't. Let me illustrate. Take a few seconds and look at this picture of the Cribb Estate in Missouri.

Cribb Estate

Cool, isn't it? In the blink of an eye you saw:

- The precise layout of 18 roof lines and all the doo-dads sticking out of them
- The placement, shape, and relative size of 30 windows
- The weird shapes of two pools
- The pool chairs, umbrellas, and tables
- The precise width of the stairs
- The placement and look of dozens of trees and shrubs
- And so much more

Hundreds of bits of data in a flash.

Now imagine you need to help someone else see that exact image but can only use your words to get them to imagine it.

Yeah. Ain't gonna happen.

You can talk for hours, but you know they're not going to get it right. None of the people who read your text will see the same thing. And to top it off, each person will imagine things you don't even tell them about. They will literally make stuff up.

All this means they won't come close unless they probably begin to draw it, and you give them feedback. And that's because reading is different than seeing. There's a reason for the saying that a picture is worth a thousand words.

When we write, we are not showing anything. We are helping the reader imagine.

But that's not all. Our working memory is limited. It can only hold around seven to nine items at a time. When we have to start manipulating those items like we do when we perform addition or comparison, it drops down to somewhere around two to four. So not only are we triggering the reader's imagination, we only have so many working memory slots to use.

All of this has significant implications for how to make things vivid and clear to readers. Chief among those implications is that less is frequently more. You will learn more about how to go about that in the course on writing chapters that transport readers. What you need to know here is that you don't need three-book histories of your character.

Your characters are brought to life mostly by what they think, say, and do—how they act and react, and the motives behind the actions. You develop a lot of that when you actually write the novel. But there's one piece you want to capture now if you can. And that's the type of person they are. This will tell you how, in general, they will approach their role in the story. And you'll capture that in a way that takes into account the fact that we're imagining, not seeing, and that we have a limited working memory.

TYPES

Our miracle brain sorts everything we come in contact with into some type. Accurate or not, types tell us what to expect. For example, if it's a dog, we're going to sort it into a type—a mean dog, a happy dog, a sneaky dog, or one of those yappy small dogs that you sometimes want to punt. We immediately type the dog and act accordingly.

We don't look at a million characteristics or consult the dog's likes and detailed history. We key in on a few salient features. These form the dominant impression of the animal. With that impression we categorize what we're seeing. And that immediately recalls other things we associate with that type. Our brain is one big categorization machine. And each category has details, expectations, and a general feel associated with it.

What we do with dogs, we also do with people, places, and things. And one of the secrets of making characters vivid and clear is to recognize how the brain processes information and work with it instead of against it. So we're going to work with the fact that the brain thinks in types and has a limited working memory.

The two chief ways we do this is by keeping the character simple and exaggerating their traits. These two things work with the brain, and because of that they help both the author and the reader imagine the character more vividly. So our character sketches are not going to go into tons a detail. They're sketches, which means they focus on the chief features.

BROAD-BRUSH + 1

One way to keep things simple is to paint a general picture of the character (broad-brush), then add in a detail or three or five that particularize them. I call this broad-brush +1. The +1 doesn't mean you must limit it to one particularization, just that you want to keep it simple. Here are some examples that should give you a feel for this approach.

Example 1. Brent is a small, fussy man who likes to iron his underwear.

In this one, "small, fussy man" paints a general picture. Ironing his underwear is a particular detail.

Example 2. Kirk is a crag of a man with a scar that runs across his throat. He also has an affinity for red roses. The scar came from his years in prison. The affinity came from the wife he lost.

"Crag of a man" is a broad-brush. The scar and rose stuff is specific.

Example 3. Melanie is a feisty teen who rides around on a pink scooter she swiped from a rich, prissy girl who thought she was everything and a bag of chips. When Mel steps onto the basketball court, she takes that attitude with her, and woe be unto the girl who tries to get position on her anywhere near the block. Although sometimes her attitude gets her into trouble—hence her black eye.

The feisty teen is the general image. The swiped pink scooter, black eye, and sports passion are the particulars.

Are these full-fledged characters? No. They're sketches. And half sketches at that. But with just the little that I've written above, you should already be getting a feel for these people.

ELEMENTS OF THE SKETCH

When sketching, I've found <u>the following elements provide the biggest bang for the buck</u>.

- <u>Dominant impression</u>
- <u>To or against type</u>
- <u>Tags</u>
- <u>Motive for helping or hindering</u>
- <u>Non-plot goal</u>
- <u>Other stuff that's relevant or cool</u>
- <u>Name</u>
- <u>Interest and rooting factors</u>

Let's look at each.

1. Dominant Impression

Some of the biggest cues we use to type folks are their <u>gender, age, vocation, and manner</u>. We also use their social class.

Gender, age, and social class are easy enough. <u>Vocation is simply the person's role in society, what they do for a living, or the role that most defines them</u>.

- Accountant
- Blowhard
- Bouncer

- Brains
- Con man
- Conspiracy theorist
- Cop
- Cowboy
- Dad
- Despot
- Drifter
- Egghead
- Fighter
- Henchman
- Hustler
- Jock
- Loner
- Martinet
- Mom
- Muscle
- Nag
- Playboy
- Spy
- Stoner
- Thief
- Vagabond
- Etc.

While it's true a person will have many roles in life, we're focusing here on the one that stands out the most. The character's chief role. We're not looking for nuance. We looking for the dominant impression.

The manner is an adjective which describes how they tend to behave. It describes the most visible part of their personality. So you have a pushy cab driver, shy basketball star, bold girl who won't be pushed around, sympathetic school teacher, drill-sergeant chef, clumsy mechanic, whiny governor, ditsy waitress, twinkle-eyed cop, forthright carpenter, shifty druggist, chatty nurse.

Here are more adjectives to help spark ideas.

- Adventurous
- Affectionate
- Aggressive
- Ambitious
- Angelic
- Avaricious
- Blunt
- Boisterous
- Brave
- Bright-eyed
- Callous
- Charming
- Chatty
- Cheerful
- Childish
- Clever
- Compassionate
- Confused
- Considerate
- Crafty
- Cranky
- Crass
- Craven
- Cruel
- Cunning
- Cynical
- Dainty
- Devil-may-care
- Dignified
- Dim-witted
- Dirty
- Dishonest
- Ditsy
- Dumpy
- Eager
- Earnest

- Easy-going
- Eccentric
- Fastidious
- Fervent
- Flighty
- Friendly
- Gentle
- Gentlemanly
- Glitzy
- Gregarious
- Grumpy
- Hard-nosed
- Hermit
- High brow
- Honest
- Honey-tongued
- Hot-headed
- Hypercritical
- Immature
- Immodest
- Industrious
- Irascible
- Jovial
- Laughing
- Lazy
- Level-headed
- Long-winded
- Loud
- Low brow
- Mean
- Meddlesome
- Mercurial
- Meticulous
- Mischievous
- Modest
- Moody

- Naive
- Nasty
- Naughty
- Nervous
- Ostentatious
- Philosophical
- Plain
- Playful
- Practical
- Quarrelsome
- Quiet
- Quick-witted
- Reclusive
- Relaxed
- Reliable
- Reserved
- Rowdy
- Rude
- Sarcastic
- Sassy
- Scrappy
- Sentimental
- Sexy
- Shy
- Silly
- Silver-tongued
- Sloppy
- Sly
- Snappy-dressing
- Sneaky
- Sniping
- Sour
- Spiteful
- Staid
- Stern
- Stoic

- Super polite
- Superficial
- Tactful
- Tactless
- Thoughtful
- Thuggish
- Tidy
- Twinkle-eyed
- Untrustworthy
- Vain
- Vulgar
- Witty
- World-weary
- World-wise
- Wasteful
- Wonky
- Zealous

There are tons of these. Use them to form a dominant impression. Keep your sketch simple and focused. If you use too many different facets to a character's personality, it will start to overload our working memory and defy our types. The result is a muddy character.

 To or Against Type

Another part of the sketch is whether the character is playing to or against type for their role. Our types lead us to expect certain things from heroes, villains, plumbers, criminals, etc. Our characters can play into those expectations or against them.

For example, is your detective a tough-guy (expected) or neurotic (unexpected)? Is your spy a deadly thirty-something male (expected) or a knitting granny (unexpected)? Is your vampire refined and alluring (expected) or redneck (unexpected)? Is your sidekick reliable (expected) or crazy (unexpected)?

Take some time to think about what you think would be cool or fun for that role. List out a bunch of options. Sometimes just one or two unexpected things will transform your characters from dull to exciting.

Tags

Until readers have spent some time with a character, they're likely to forget the type of person that character is and what they look like. This happens because we can only hold so many things in working memory. Every new paragraph we read moves info into our working memory that pushes the info from previous paragraphs out. After fifty paragraphs, we forget a lot of detail. So if you describe Barney at the beginning of the chapter as a hulking black man, it's quite possible that impression will fade. Especially if you switch to a scene that doesn't include him. The next time Barney appears the reader might think, Barney? Barney who? And then go flipping back to figure out who this Barney character is.

We don't want them flipping back. We want the characters to be vivid, clear, and immediately recognizable. One simple, but powerful technique to help readers remember and distinguish your character from the others is to give him or her a distinctive prop, way of speaking, way of dressing, physical characteristic, mannerism, or tic.

We call these things character tags. And every time you bring that character on you work one of the tags into the action. If it's a long scene, after a few pages, you can refresh the reader's imagination by salting in another tag or two as a reminder.

For example, if you have a skeletal and scary librarian, you can work in her bony hands, the thin skin on her arms that reveals the veins underneath, her face that looks like a skull, the bumps of her spine bones on her neck, etc.

If you have no-nonsense soldier from England, you can work in words like rubbish, blimey, bleeder, knickers, Mum, etc.

If you have a character who is a philosophical garbage man, you can work in his garbage man outfit and inject gnomic sayings into the conversation like "The oxen are slow, you rat-eater, but the earth is patient."

Your character might always wear a beanie or scarf or hoodie. She might carry certain types of weapons. He might be fond of whittling. She might giggle in a certain way. He might limp. She might comb her fingers through her hair. He might comb a part in such a tidy way it blows your mind. Maybe he has a bald head or bushy eyebrows. Maybe she's tiny and has tiny shoes, tiny gloves, and a tiny hat. Maybe he's monstrous and has hands like mallets and shoes the size of cinderblocks.

Eloise McGraw summed up the power of tags by saying,

> "These small habits and gestures are very important to a characterization. A couple of them, well-selected, can make a character come through more vividly than anything else you do with him. More than any other one thing, they will define and express a personality" (*Techniques of Fiction Writing* p46).

So have fun and follow the rule of cool. Come up with some distinctive tags, and help your readers imagine your characters.

4. Motive for Helping or Hindering

Your story is about a character trying to achieve a goal that was prompted by a THOM. Characters will either try to help the main character, hinder her, or perform stock functions.

For those that help and hinder, what's their motive for doing so? If it's your main character, what will be the motive for him getting involved?

Remember, you're creating a sketch to help you imagine this person and how they will approach their role. The character's motives are critical to that. Their motives can be straight-forward or complicated. Just take some time to think about it.

5. Non-plot Goal

For your main characters, you will probably find it helpful to get a feel for them if you know what their main non-plot goal or enjoyment is.

If you look back at those examples of Roxie, she was interested in enjoying her granddaughter, or making money to help her daughter

Create Story Ideas that Beg to be Written

with cancer. <u>These non-plot goals help make her more sympathetic and put more at stake</u>.

But you don't always have to use goals or enjoyments that make the character sympathetic. They can also suggest cool skills that could be used in the story. Maybe Roxie loves rebuilding cars; maybe she loves sky diving and broke her leg and just wants to do one more jump; maybe she loves sailing.

Whatever you decide to use, non-plot goals, enjoyments, and activities help round out a character, suggest a larger life, <u>and can provide possibilities for the story</u>.

 Other Stuff That's Relevant or Cool

You do not need to know the character's favorite food, his first pet, or even the name of his mother. You don't need to know your character's greatest fear, weakness, history, political party, attitude towards hamburgers, or a hundred other things.

Why?

Because we want to make characters that are memorable and interesting, and the name of the summer camp your character went to when she was eight doesn't really affect that. Unless, of course, the camp was a spy training camp run by the CIA, and it taught her how to use a garrote.

<u>Fulsome character histories and lists of likes and dislikes are not necessary</u>. I'm not saying that writing them is wrong. I'm simply saying <u>it's not necessary</u>.

However, <u>if you want to add some anecdote from your character's past because it's cool, do it</u>. So maybe the born-again teacher used to be a stripper. And maybe her knowledge of that stripper world will help her in her mystery plot.

Maybe the Army sergeant used to drive teams of Clydesdales when he worked on a Montana ranch. And he uses his knowledge of horses to steal some in the desert when he and his platoon of men get lost.

Maybe the prankster grandpa used to hunt rattlesnakes with his bare hands. And maybe that might help him in the action plot. Or maybe not. Maybe you want him to know how to handle rattlesnakes because it's awesome, and you have no idea how he might use it until you're writing the chapters.

If it's cool or relevant to the story, great. If it's not cool or relevant, don't bother. This is a sketch that's simply trying to help you clearly envision what the character is like and how they'll approach their role in the story so you can write them. Anything that doesn't help with that only clutters up the picture.

 Name

Names and nicknames are wonderful tools for evoking or working against a type and telling us something about the character.

If I tell you a character's name is Penelope, you'll imagine someone different than if I tell you her name is Lashonda, Guadalupe, Anne, or Leviticus. Frank will make you imagine one thing. Benjamin Childs may make you think of another.

Tiny might be the nickname of a tiny guy or a huge one. Legs might be a nickname of someone who is fast or refer to some funny incident in the character's past that can be revealed later on in the plot.

Think about the name or nickname and ask yourself if it works for what you're doing with this character. As always, have fun and follow the rule of cool.

 Interest and Rooting Factors

By this point you've probably already sketched yourself an interesting character. If not, it's time to review the things that generate character interest and see if there's something you can use to boost the effect. That doesn't mean you have to use a multiplicity of interest factors and make your character a good-looking, ninja billionaire with secrets. Unless, of course, you want to do Batman. Also, if it's the main character, you will want to check to make sure they are the type that will fall on the deserving side of the justice meter.

USEFUL TRICKS

One thing that that helps many authors capture the essence of a character is to <u>associate them with a picture of a person, place, or thing. Another is to use a metaphor</u>. <u>A third is to base them on some other person or character</u>.

Jack's a crag of a man, a shrimp of a man, strong as a horse, a snake. Mary's a wraith, a bulldozer, the Rock of Gibraltar. Juan is like Clint Eastwood's character in High Plains Drifter. Sharmala is like my Aunt Edna. This picture of Roxie is perfect for kick-butt granny. The picture you just found of a rusted-out Ford pickup captures the feel of your character perfectly.

Pictures, metaphors, and exemplars can all be very helpful because <u>they all embody some type</u>. So feel free to use them to help you sketch your character.

FINAL THOUGHTS

There's no one way to write up your sketch. You can use bullets. You can write it out in paragraph form. The purpose of the sketch is to clarify the character in your mind. <u>You should probably keep the sketch shorter rather than longer.</u> What's the ideal size? I don't know that there is one. I've written a sketch of a main character in two sentences. Others have taken longer.

<u>What you want to remember is that your fictional characters are not *homo sapiens*. They are *homo fictus*</u>. And you are trying to work with the mind to <u>evoke them in both yours and your reader's imagination. Usually, this means you need to make them both more exaggerated and simpler than real human beings.</u> I've always found this statement by Dwight V. Swain helpful.

> "It's also important to remember that <u>making a character too complex will kill him. A good character is a simulation of complexity</u>, not the real thing. <u>Fairly clear and simple traits work best.</u> Otherwise the effect will be that given by a 'busy' painting, one too cluttered with detail. So while ordinarily you'll want to go beyond the cartoon/caricature level, try not

to carry development so far in depth that your people fall over the edge into total confusion. The meaningful character in fiction is the one with a salient feature, or two or three, like the real-life Ayatollah Khomeini, Richard Nixon, or Elvis Presley, with individuality and color added via modifying touches." (*Creating Characters* p21).

Remember: your characters truly come alive when they think, speak, and do on the page. The sketch is simply a tool to evoke the type of person they are and how they're going to approach their role and interact with the other characters in the story so you know how to write them.

Of course, if we just wanted to capture characters, we'd take up painting or photography. Novels aren't about characters. They're about characters with THOMs—**T**hreats, **H**ardships, **O**pportunities, and **M**ysteries. And in the next chapter you'll learn a few secrets about how to make those THOMs more compelling.

8

AWESOME THOMS AND GOALS

We have tons of mule deer up where I live, and they do something interesting every time I come upon them. As soon as they see, smell, or hear me, they run for twenty or thirty yards, stop, then turn and look back at me.

Are they taunting me? No, they're not that clever. And thank heavens for that. Can you imagine being inundated with prankster deer? I have enough problems in my yard with their current level of intelligence. In this instance, their motives are much more basic. Staying alive is a big deal to them. It's a primal impulse. They perceive me as a possible threat, and so they put some distance between themselves and me, then turn to keep track of me because no deer in its right mind wants to ignore a predator.

However, fleeing isn't the only response deer make. My father had some pet sika deer when he was a kid. When he appeared, instead of fleeing, his deer would hustle over to him because he usually had apples or sugar cubes in his pocket. In this situation they wanted to keep him in sight, not because he was a threat, but because he represented a delicious opportunity. It was a primal response.

Deer will also respond with an alerting response when they

encounter something new. There's a drive to figure out if the thing is going to be a threat, opportunity, or neither.

Humans are the same as those deer. We care about things that affect our primal needs. And the THOM simply describes those needs. It's no accident that our stories revolve around these things.

COMPELLING STORIES FOCUS ON HUMAN NEEDS

I break the THOM down into two categories. The THO focuses our desire to survive and thrive. We humans are wired to constantly scan our environment for things that we think will make us happy and those that present a danger to that happiness.

When we see something we think will make us happy like a delicious roasted turkey dinner with all the fixings, a cool car, or a good friend, we become alert and focus on it. When we see something we think will undercut our happiness or cause us suffering, we do the same. If humans didn't do this, we would have all been eaten by lions, fallen off cliffs, or starved to death long ago. The interesting thing is that we're also wired to react in a similar way when others, like characters in a book, face these things.

While the THO revolve around primal happiness needs, the M focuses on our desire to figure out our surroundings. We're curious creatures. And that's a good thing because our curiosity leads us to figure out what can make us happy, what poses a threat, and what doesn't matter. Presenting a strange situation (mystery) to the reader, especially if it has to do with things that affect happiness, piques their interest. Of course, sometimes discovery all by itself is enough.

Let's look at some examples of THOMs so you can more easily generate options for your stories. We can break the happiness needs the THO revolves around into three categories: physical, social, self-fulfillment.

Physical

These needs have to do with survival, health, security, and control of property. When we see a threat to or opportunity for them, or are experiencing a lack of one of them (hardship), we get interested. So you have these types of stories.

- **Monster.** Stop the monster, catch the monster, escape the monster. The monster might be a monster. Or it could be a kidnapper, slaver, assassin, crime lord, virus, velociraptor, killer storm, asteroid, etc. Whatever it is, <u>it's threatening you or someone else physically</u>.
- **Treasure.** Find the treasure, steal the treasure, keep the treasure. The treasure might be Spanish gold, but it also might be a car, a fountain of youth, a patent, an oil well in the back yard, a stud bull, etc. <u>It's anything that would help us with our wealth or health.</u>
- **Recovery.** Recover from a terrible loss in one of these areas.

Here are some examples.

- You're wounded, trapped on a rock a hundred meters from the beach with the tide raising the water and a huge shark scenting your blood. You need to kill or escape the monster.
- Bullies are stealing your money, roughing you up, and making your life miserable.
- You're in zombie territory and want to get to safety. You need to evade and escape the monsters.
- Your daughter has contracted a disease that might affect her vision. You need to stop this monster.
- You have been laid off from work and will lose the house and be tossed out on the street if you don't find another job quickly. You need to find a treasure.
- A despot is gathering armies to conquer and enslave your community. You want to stop the monster.
- Someone has been murdered and the killer is still on the loose. You want to catch and stop the monster.
- A gang is looking for you to teach you a lesson. You want to stop or escape them.

- A thief has stolen your life savings. You want to get the treasure back.
- The smog is affecting your son's health and you decide to see if you can make it in the country. You want to escape this hardship.
- You lost all your money in a stock market crash and struggle to rebuild it.

Physical needs drive so many stories.

Social

These needs have to do with love and belonging. They include things like friendship, intimacy, family, sense of connection, respect, status, recognition, and reputation. When we see a threat to or opportunity for them, or are experiencing a lack of one of them (hardship), we get interested. So you have these types of stories.

- **Romance.** Find romance, rebuild a broken romance, keep a romance. Anything that presents an opportunity for romance or threatens an existing one.
- **Familial love.** Develop familial love, rebuild a broken familial love, keep a familial love.
- **Buddy.** Find a friend, rebuild a broken friendship, keep a friendship.
- **Enemy.** Make an enemy a friend, make a friend an enemy.
- **Acceptance.** Face ostracism, find acceptance, win respect or admiration, develop a good reputation, keep your reputation.
- **Recovery.** Recover from a terrible loss in one of these areas.

Here are some examples.

- You're single and meet someone you could fall in love with and marry. That story has been told a million times.
- Your spouse leaves you, and you want to win her back.
- The joy in your marriage seems to have left.

- You and your spouse want to have children but can't. You want to have these great treasures called children.
- You are teamed up with someone who you don't like very much, or just plain drives you nuts, and by the end you become friends. A very common buddy story.
- Your child is being ostracized at school.
- You have to go to war. You want to make sure you stay alive so you can return and enjoy your wife and kids.
- Someone has accused you of a despicable thing. Everyone in the community is turning against you.

We're interested in belonging. In fact, it's so interesting to us that we often add a social story as a subplot to those focusing on physical needs.

Self-fulfillment

These needs have to do with us meeting our potential. They include things like having self-respect, feeling our life has a purpose, rising to a level of mastery, and enjoying freedom. When we see a threat to or opportunity for them, or are experiencing a lack of one of them (hardship), we get interested. So you have these types of stories.

- **Freedom.** Keep freedom, win freedom.
- **Self-worth.** Discover self-worth, regain self-worth (redemption stories), keep self-worth (temptation stories).
- **Purpose.** Escape drudgery, maintain ability to live a meaningful life, fulfil a dream.
- **Mastery.** Succeed at your endeavor. A lot of sports stories feature this.
- **Recovery.** Recover from a terrible loss in one of these areas.

Here are some examples.

- You work in a job full of drudgery and see an opportunity to do something that makes your heart sing.
- You sacrificed time with your son in the past for work, missed

out on so many things in his life, and are now seeking to set things right.
- You're a soldier and ran in cowardice and want to regain your self-respect.
- You work at a job with a manager who is constantly running you down.
- You get a chance to go to a wizard school and learn magic.

We all love a good story where a character finds meaning in their life.

Discovery

This need has to do with figuring things out. When something odd is going on, we want to explain it. When there are secrets, we want to know them. When there is a suspected threat, we want to know what it is. There's a thrill in puzzling out odd situations and unraveling mysteries.

- You hear ethereal sounds in the woods at night.
- You come outside to find your tools scattered three nights in a row, but know it's impossible that anyone has been in your yard.
- You swear you can hear voices in the walls of your house.
- Something odd has appeared in the sky.
- You start to receive gifts from an anonymous benefactor.

Mystery can also add interest to a THO story because a lack of knowledge can act as an obstacle to us removing threats, resolving hardships, and seizing opportunities. Think about a murder mystery. Those stories are about bringing an evil-doer to justice and restoring security. But the main obstacle isn't catching the person. The main obstacle is figuring out who did it and why. Once the detective figures that out, catching and bringing the person to justice is usually very easy. Here are some examples of this.

- Your child contracts are rare disease without a cure, and then you stumble onto a possible lead.
- Your cattle are dying and not from disease, and then you find a clue that someone or something is coming into your fields at night.
- National secrets are falling into the hands of enemies, and then you discover the source is a mole in your agency.
- Your friend is acting strangely. You go to find out what's going on, and see her talking to some rough-looking men.
- You met a wonderful woman, but lost her contact information. All you know is that she lives in Los Angeles.

So the mystery can be the main course, or it can be part of figuring out what's going on or the key to defeating the antagonist.

The Rule of Cool

If you look at the needs above, you'll notice that there's an element of wish-fulfillment to many of them.

- Wouldn't it be awesome to have the opportunity to earn a million bucks?
- Wouldn't it be cool to be on such an adventure?
- Wouldn't it be awesome to fall in love with such a person?
- Wouldn't it be awesome to have such a marriage?
- Wouldn't it be cool to see those lights coming out of our sewers?

Sometimes thinking about what would be cool can lead you to the THOM as well.

THOM Combinations

As you saw in the previous examples, many stories might combine elements of the THOM.

For example, a group of youth might be discriminated against (social hardship), have an opportunity as a sports team to achieve mastery (self-fulfillment opportunity), and win acceptance from others at their school as they struggle and succeed (social opportunity). In another story, a tough operator might be trying to figure out which evil organization (mystery) is killing people with some new man-made virus (physical threat).

You can have stories that combine all sorts of THOMs. The point of this chapter is not to define every possible combination. Or to suggest there's some secret combination that leads to success. The point of this chapter is to make sure you recognize that some form of THOM is required to start the story. Until you have a THOM, you don't have a story.

Identify Your Main THOM

Whatever combination you cook up, it is important to identify what the main THOM is. Knowing this will help you know where to begin your novel and where to end it. The way you do this is simple. Look at the THOM you've created and ask yourself which issue, when resolved, ends the story.

For example, look at the killer virus story above. Is the story over when the operator figures out who is dispersing the virus? No. The threat still remains. The story is over when the people have been stopped and the outbreak or epidemic contained.

Look at the story of the rag-tag sports team. When is that one over? Well, if I was interested most about them developing self-respect despite what others thought, it might be when they win the championship, even if they don't gain wide acceptance. If I was most interested in a story about a community accepting those who are different, the team might lose the championship, but find acceptance.

Knowing the main THOM at the heart of your story is important. It helps you see what you need to focus on, discover the formidable obstacle that will stand in the way, and structure the events of your story.

Create Story Ideas that Beg to be Written

② How Did We Get Here?

Some THOMs don't have an interesting backstory. They just appear. For example, one day Bill is happy. And then at 3:23 p.m. scientists discover a hunk of ice and stone six miles across hurtling toward Earth. A hunk as big as the one that took the dinosaurs out. And it's projected to hit in the Montana wilderness, right where his daughter is backpacking without any electronics.

Other THOMs do have a backstory of events that lead up to the moment the hero comes on stage. For example, in murder mysteries, there are all sorts of things that happen before the detective gets involved. It's vital to know why the person was murdered, how, and by whom. And what the murderer's plan is to get away with it.

Think about your THOM. Is there a backstory to it? If there's a villain involved, the villain is almost always already pursuing his goal. What is that goal? Why is he pursuing it? What's his plan to get it? And what has he already put into motion?

Other THOMs could be the result of something the hero did in the past. For example, maybe the hero put some mob boss's daughter in jail. And now the mob boss is coming after him. Or maybe the hero showed someone mercy, and now that person is out killing people. Or maybe it's a story in which an estranged father and son have to work together to beat the bad guys. And while the external story is about beating the bad guys, the real story is about these two men reconciling their differences. If so, why is there bad blood between them?

Look at your THOM and ask: what led to the current situation? Look for cool conflicts, events, and secrets. Try to work some zing into it. A good backstory can often make your front story more delicious.

INCREASE READER INTEREST WITH URGENCY

The THOM focuses on core human needs, but we won't care much if the problems aren't urgent. Here are some ways to increase the urgency.

1. Increase the Probability of the Negative Outcome

It's one thing to think that yeah, sure, there's a minuscule chance of being hit by an asteroid. It's quite another to know an asteroid is on a 100%-certain collision course with the planet. The higher the probability of the threat or loss of opportunity, the more intense the problem becomes because it's more likely to affect our needs. No probability and I have nothing to fear.

2. Make the Issue More Immediate

It's one thing to know that asteroid will hit the earth and wipe us out in 7,000 years. It's quite another to know it will hit tomorrow.

The more immediate the problem, the less likely I'll be able to solve it. The less likely my chances are, the more I'll worry. Give us 7,000 years, and I'm sure we'll figure out the asteroid thing. Give us twenty-four hours, and that's probably cutting it too close. This is why setting up a time limit, a ticking clock or ticking time-bomb, can ratchet up the audience's tension. Of course, it has to be a short time limit. You can't start the bomb ticking, and give the hero forty-five years to disarm it.

3. Increase the Stakes

It's one thing to face the kidnapping of my pet spider. It's quite another to face the kidnapping of my child. The more that's put at risk, the more we care. Remember, this doesn't have to be physical risk. You can put a delightful relationship between a daughter and father or daughter and mother at risk. You can put the character in a situation that risks a life of drudgery. There are fates worse than death.

4. Make It More Specific

It's one thing to say that something bad is going to happen. It's quite another to know that kidnappers are going to cut your finger off with a pair of wire cutters. It's one thing to have someone say something good will happen to you and quite another to say your uncle just died and left you a million dollars.

Humans are wired to respond to concrete details far more than they are to abstractions. The more specific the problem, the easier it is for us to see the specific possibilities and react to them with hope and fear. Generalities don't trigger emotions. Striking snakes do, though. As do garbage disposals that are turned on just when you reach in to get the baby's pacifier.

5. Bring the Threat Close to Home

Another intensifier is to make the threat specific to the hero. It's one thing to say a lot of people in the United States or Russia or India are going to die. It's another to say the hero will lose his own child or wife in the event. A flood raging in the next county is different than the one coming down our street.

This is not to say you can't write about threats to large groups of people. That's one of the ways to broaden the scope of the problem and make it more significant. It's just that problems become more intense the closer they come to home. Things that threaten us personally, or those we love, raise more fears than those that threaten people we don't know. The more personal you make the threat to the character, the more intense the threat will be.

INCREASE READER INTEREST WITH RELEVANCE

Another way to increase reader interest is to make sure the situation is relevant to the reader or has an attractive draw.

Make Sure the Issue Resonates With the Target Audience

While there is huge overlap in the specific threats, hardships, and opportunities people care about, there are also differences. For example, some issues that matter to middle-grade readers aren't always the same ones as those that matter to adults. Some of the issues that attract males aren't always the same ones that attract females. Some of the issues that matter to people in one social class or group don't always matter as much to those in another. One audience might be more interested in relationship issues, another might be more interested in physical threats. One might be more interested in redemption, another more interested in high school romance. One might be drawn to stories about lost unicorns, others are more interested in war. Think about your audience and make sure you think the issue will resonate with them.

Add an Element of Wish-fulfillment

Do you remember the list of things that make characters compelling? One of those things is having the character be, do, or have something we find attractive or exciting. Spies are exciting. So are pirates and magical abilities. There are lots of situations we would love to be in. We'd love to live like the wealthy, go on a Medieval adventure, fall in love, or learn how to be a soldier. There are other situations we might not necessarily want to experience in real life but that are exciting to think about. And so one way to increase reader interest is to make the situation the character finds themselves in something attractive or exciting.

MAKE DEALING WITH THE THOM UNAVOIDABLE

If our character could just walk away and avoid all the risks, dangers, and troubles of a problem, we would expect them to do so. Of course, if they do, there goes our story. So we must devise good reasons why the hero can't or won't walk away. Normally, it will involve one or more of the following reasons:

- Physical
- Moral
- Professional

Physical reasons are simply those that physically force people into facing the problem. The hero is stuck on an island with a monster and can't physically get away. She is on an airplane thousands of feet up with terrorists and can't physically leave. She is on a ship when it begins

Create Story Ideas that Beg to be Written

to sink. She's behind enemy lines. The villain wants her dead and seems to have no problem finding her. In these situations, something physical is preventing the character from avoiding the problem. It doesn't matter whether she wants to solve the problem or not, she's going to have to deal with it.

On the other hand, there are situations where our characters have a choice.

The character might have strong moral reasons that compel him to face the problem. Maybe a child is in danger. In this situation, the hero does something bad by not acting. Maybe someone he loves will be hurt or die if he fails to deal with the issue. He can choose to walk away, but the moral costs would be too high.

A character might also choose to engage the problem for professional reasons. These characters try to solve problems because it's their job. Cops track down killers. Soldiers go into war. Bounty hunters chase folks that jump bail.

Any one or combination of these reasons is sufficient.

Please note that presenting a reason why the character can't walk away applies to relationship stories as well. If you want a relationship to build, the people involved need to spend time with each other, and so there must be something that forces them to be with each other. The two people might be stranded together in the wilderness or forced to work together on a project or a team. They might be working against each other on some issue like opposing lawyers do. Whatever it is, they need a reason to be together.

In all stories, you can present the reasons why the hero can't walk away at the same time the THOM is introduced, or you can present it in a separate scene. Also, you can vary your hero's initial reaction. Sometimes the hero is motivated from the get-go and takes one paragraph to decide to tackle the problem head-on. But sometimes the hero is reluctant or even unwilling and needs a shove. In such cases, it might require an additional scene or two to give her the necessary motivation.

However you choose to approach it, you need to come up with a reason why your hero must deal with the THOM.

THE GOAL, TO GAIN OR RETAIN

Once you introduce a THOM and reason why the character can't walk away, you must establish what important thing the character is going to try to gain or retain. If you don't establish a clear goal, there is no story.

Imagine someone is murdered, but nobody decides to figure out who did it and bring them to justice. That turns your story into a crime-scene photograph.

Imagine your character is trapped in an enclosure with a velociraptor but doesn't decide to escape. It turns your story into a presentation of lunch.

The THOM triggers hopes and fears for the characters and curiosity. It also triggers a desire to see those hopes and fears and curiosity resolved. But if you don't state or imply a clear goal, the readers can't root for the character to succeed because there's nothing the character is striving for.

The other thing you have to keep in mind is that concrete specifics move us more than abstractions do. The general goal of fighting crime appeals to us less than the specific goal of stopping the Kuz gang that gunned down Paul, the kid in our neighborhood who rakes our leaves each autumn.

The general goal of being happy moves you less than the specific goal of getting a desperately needed $500 to pay the rent by asking the construction company down the road if they'll hire you.

The general goal of survival sparks your imagination less than the specific goal of mixing your poop in the dirt and see if you can get bacteria to grow so you can raise a crop of potatoes so you don't starve in your Mars habitat.

Some people ask me if this goal is at play in romances. It is. Sometimes the character's goal is to win the affection of the boy or girl. But sometimes it's just the opposite. In these cases, the THOM is an attraction, an opportunity for something good, but the character decides following that attraction and falling in love is the wrong thing to do. And so the character's goal is to resist the attraction. Of course, because the two characters are forced to be with one another, that isn't so easy.

After you develop a THOM, state or clearly imply the specific end goal. Then flip it into a story question that can be answered with a yes or no. When you do, you can then come up with formidable obstacles to reaching that goal. And those obstacles will create the delicious uncertainty and suspense readers crave.

THE INCITING INCIDENT

Your story starts when the THOM is introduced into the character's life. We sometimes call that the inciting incident because it incites your character to action. Or at least incites the need for action, even if the character at first decides he or she wants nothing to do with it.

We'll cover this more in the course on creating outlines, but you'll notice that even at this point in the story development stage, your mind will start to imagine the specifics of how the THOM is introduced to the character's life. If you start to get ideas for the events in the tale, including the inciting incident, great! Write them down. If not, don't sweat it. You'll figure it out when you take the course on developing your outline.

One last point. Urgent needs and goals aren't enough. Remember: there are five elements in the story setup. And we don't have a story until we have formidable obstacles. In fact, it's obstacles that allow us to build the anxiety, anticipation, and curiosity that readers go to our stories to enjoy. And we'll cover that in the next chapter.

9

FORMIDABLE OBSTACLES

A cake just isn't a cake without the sugar. You can have all the flour, butter, vanilla, baking powder, milk, and cocoa you want, but if the sugar ain't there, it ain't a cake.

Likewise, you can have heaps 'o character, mind-blowing THOMs, stunning locations, and a terrific cast. But it you don't have obstacles, you don't have a story. <u>Formidable obstacles are the sugar in your story cake</u>.

Don't believe me? Try this version of *The Lord of the Rings*.

Gandalf motions at the ring in Frodo's hand. "The Dark Lord is seeking it. All his will is bent on it. If he gets it, it will be the end of Hobbiton. It will be the end of the world."

Frodo holds the ring out to him. "Take it, Gandalf. Destroy it."

"No! It will eat my lunch. My little friend, you must destroy the ring. You're the only one who can do it."

"Okay," Frodo says. And then he scampers into the hallway, out the door, across the road, and casts the ring into the tanner's boiling tub of water. The water dissolves the ring and releases some gas. And far to the east lighting flashes and the Dark Lord falls to ruins.

Frodo walks back to the kitchen where Gandalf waits. "Well, that's done. Are you ready for second breakfast?"

Create Story Ideas that Beg to be Written

The end.

What a terrific story. Do you think anyone will pay me $9.99 for it? Do you think it will get a movie deal?

No, I didn't think so either.

This begs the question: what is *The Lord of the Rings*? Yes, there's a nice stay in Rivendell, an attractive and dangerous elvish woman named Galadriel, and some moments with tobacco and singing. Yes, we have a boatload of cool characters. But the vast majority of the story is not about the characters sitting around a campfire being characters. The vast majority is about the obstacles they face while pursuing their THOM-triggered goals. The vast majority is about big, old, nasty obstacles.

Dealing with obstacles makes up the vast majority of any story.

Readers don't want to know what *will* happen. They want to know what *might* happen and worry about the possibilities. They want that tension to build, and then they want to feel a cathartic release.

Readers don't want to know what the answer to the mystery *will* be. They want to feel the curiosity of a puzzle. They want that mystery to get weirder and more puzzling; they want the gotta-know feeling to build and build; and then they want a cathartic release.

You build that desire in readers by leaving the story question unresolved. How do we make sure this desire persists and intensifies for forty to seventy scenes (an average range for many novels) despite the character's best efforts?

Obstacles.

That means the danger isn't removed; it gets worse. The hardship isn't resolved; it grows. The mystery becomes more and more confounding. Yes, the hero will have some successes along the way, but there's always another obstacle. The goal is always in jeopardy.

Your story has a job to do, which means you can't have your characters go about solving the problem in any old way. Form follows function. You have to develop the plot in a manner that builds the tension readers crave. And we do this by making it harder for the character to reach the goal that was prompted by the THOM. When we do that, we create uncertainty. And up and down uncertainty takes the reader on a rollercoaster ride of hopes, fears, and mystery.

So let's look at different types of difficulties you can use in your stories.

1. DISADVANTAGES

The first way we make the problem hard to solve is by putting the character at a disadvantage. The disadvantage may be a small, medium, or large, depending on your taste and the kind of story you're telling. There isn't one type or level that's best for all stories. But our characters do have to have some disadvantage; otherwise, there's no reason for readers to fear they'll fail to gain or retain what they're trying to achieve.

a. Lack of Knowledge

One of the most common disadvantages is a character starting off not knowing how to solve the problem. Or not having a critical piece of information that will allow them to solve it.

For example, think of all the murder mysteries you've read or seen. The character starts off not knowing who the killer is or why they did it. If it's a kidnapping of a daughter, the father or mother will not know who kidnapped his daughter or where they'd taken her. Usually, the heroes have all the skills and power needed to resolve the issue once they answer the questions. What they lack are vital bits of information.

Sometimes the characters think they know what the problem is, but when they try to solve it, they realize they didn't really know what the problem was. It's called misdiagnosis.

For example, in one story the hero might think his problem is a rogue robot. But when he defeats it, he realizes he was wrong. There's something else behind the robot. In another story, a man might think his problem is that his wife is stepping out on him. When he tries to resolve that, he learns she's actually being blackmailed. A man might start off thinking he's being threatened by people who want to get to his brother's money. But when he tries to solve that problem, he realizes that it's a plot by his brother to kill him.

Any time your character doesn't know how to solve the problem or doesn't know the exact nature of the problem, it makes the problem harder to solve.

Lack of Skills or Power ✘

You can make a problem harder to solve by <u>limiting the character's skill or power in some way</u>.

Luke Skywalker knows the Death Star is going to blow a whole planet into smithereens. We have no question about what's going on. Luke knows what he needs to do—start an explosive chain reaction that will destroy the thing. So Luke has all the information he needs. What Luke lacks is the power to easily go in and execute the plan. He doesn't have his own death ray. He doesn't have computers that seem to be able to target with the precision he needs. All he's got is a dinky little X-wing fighter. He's limited in his ability.

Here's another example. Let's say a Jewish woman is taken by the Nazis. Her lover, who is a German soldier, wants to rescue her. But the lover has no power to order the men to release her. He has no money to pay them off. This doesn't mean he can't rescue her. But it does mean he's going to have to find some other way. It means resolving the issue is going to become much harder.

Flaws and Misbeliefs

Sometimes personality flaws or misbeliefs about life, people, and things can put the hero at a disadvantage. In fact, some stories are about a character overcoming the flaw or misbelief.

Maybe the hero is recovering from an addiction to some drug and finds himself being required to snort a line in front of the villain to prove he's legit. Maybe he's a male chauvinist and won't accept the help of a woman, but she's the only one with the key to resolving the story problem. Maybe he's too proud to admit he's wrong. Maybe he's a slob and loses things, including the key to the getaway car. Maybe he doesn't know when to stop drinking. Maybe his lack of self-control leads him to follow after a woman who comes on to him and then leads him right into the hands of the villain. Maybe he lacks social graces, but needs to fake high-class manners to infiltrate the villain's circles. Maybe the character has an issue with trust, has been burned too many times, and begins to suspect the other team members.

Maybe the character's virtue is the source of his flaw. He's so willing to see the good in people he blinds himself to who the villain really is. She's so committed to doing her duty that she's sacrificing her chance at a loving relationship for it.

Of course, flaws affect our sense of deservingness too. Take personality flaws too far and our hero will become annoying or despicable. You don't want your reader shouting at the book, "Are you kidding me! I hate that guy!" At that point, the reader stops rooting and worrying for them. Still, flaws can be a rich mine for making the problem harder to solve.

d. Handicaps

If all a character needs to do is snap his fingers to solve the problem, then readers can't worry for him. Unless, of course, he's missing fingers. Handicaps can put our characters at a disadvantage.

Sometimes the handicap is physical. In *Seabiscuit*, the jockey is blind in one eye. This makes it very difficult during a race to see when someone is riding up on his blind side. It also makes it hard for him to see openings ahead. It puts him at a disadvantage in a race. In the movie *Wait Until Dark*, three criminals threaten a woman who is blind. In *Gattica*, the hero has DNA that makes him weaker than the others wanting to travel into space.

In other stories, the handicaps might be emotional, mental, or social. In *Forrest Gump*, the hero is mentally handicapped. In *Iron Man 3*, Iron Man needs to fight but is suffering from PTSD. In the Monk series, the detective suffers from obsessive-compulsive disorder. Imagine trying to escape someone who is chasing you when you feel like you must touch each post along the sidewalk as you run. In other stories, heroes are tormented by fears of snakes, spiders, being alone.

Handicaps can be interesting all by themselves, but when they become a disadvantage to the hero's goal of solving the problem, they help us create tension.

ⓔ **Time Limits**

Another disadvantage is having a time limit. Of course, a time limit of a gazillion years doesn't make problems harder to solve. We want time limits and ticking time bombs that don't allow enough time to solve the problem by normal means.

Next time you read a book or watch a movie, notice how many deadlines, ticking clocks, and time bombs are used.

ⓕ **We Want Underdogs!**

When do you cheer more? When your non-ranked, underdog sports team beats the number one team in the nation, or when your champs slaughter the local pee-wees?

We love rooting for underdogs! Why? In part, because of the uncertainty.

Therefore, the disadvantages our characters have are only useful if they make the character the underdog when compared to the opposition. Our hero can have all sorts of great qualities, and we want them to be exceptional in some way, but the opposition must have something that gives them the advantage. They need to be two or three steps ahead. They need more money, more power, more knowledge, more connections, more training, more of whatever is important in the story.

For example, in *Raiders of the Lost Ark*, Indiana Jones has mad adventure-guy skills and archaeological knowledge, but he's outnumbered, outgunned, and out-financed. And the Nazis always seem to be a step ahead. In Dean Koontz's *The Good Guy*, the hero has great combat skills, but it's just him against the U.S. government. In *The Lord of the Rings*, we've got a wizard who can work wonders and an elf that can see and hear for miles. But Sauron has so much more. By the end, all we are left with are two little guys and a smelly freak job.

The opposition's advantage doesn't always have to be huge. Sometimes the hero is the underdog simply because he starts two or three steps behind the villain. In fact, the first part of many stories features the hero just trying to catch up.

The point is that making the hero an underdog allows readers to fear for her. And when she wins, it makes her victory that much sweeter.

CONFLICTS

Conflict occurs when two entities with active wills have goals that oppose each other.

- The antagonist and his henchmen want to steal the money. The hero wants to prevent that money from being stolen.
- The hero needs to sneak behind enemy lines, but the artificial intelligence is set up to prevent such intrusions.
- The dog wants to protect its territory, but the hero needs to enter that territory to get a critical clue.
- The hero sets a trap to catch the villain at a Subway restaurant, but one of the guys on the hero's team has a son with some terrible disease. And the traitor figures he can get the money he needs if he sells the hero out to the bad guys.

You can have conflicts between:

- The hero and the bad guys
- The hero and one or more of the good guys
- The hero and a bit character
- The hero and other intelligent things like robots and animals
- The hero and herself

Let's look at each.

With the Opposition

Your character will have points of conflict with the opposition. That's a given. The smarter and more powerful the opposition, the harder the problem is to solve, the more the reader can worry, and the bigger the triumph at the end. So you want to make your opposition character and team a real threat.

Create Story Ideas that Beg to be Written

The best way I've found to do this is to play the story as one-man chess, thinking not just about the hero, but about the opposition as well. The hero is, for the opposition, a problem. And so I've found it very productive to develop the opposition's goal, motives, and plan. The hero makes a move, and then I turn the table and ask: what cunning, smart, or scary reactions might this opposition character have to what the hero just did? Back and forth I go, letting both characters act with as much intelligence and cunning as they possess.

Remember, the better the opposition, the more tension the reader will feel because a formidable opponent increases the chances in the reader's mind that the hero will fail.

With the Other Good Guys

Sometimes we think only about the opposition, but the other good guys can provide many delicious conflicts. In fact, if you think about casting variety, this is just an extension of that topic.

So maybe the hero is about to break a moral code some of the other good guys won't, or vice versa.

Maybe a key player on the team just can't stand the risk.

Maybe one of the good guys loses the vision and turns traitor.

Maybe the good guys have different reasons for being on the team. One guy joins the army because the judge told him he could join the army or join the convicts in the big house. Another guy joins because he feels a duty and all of the men in his family have served since the Civil War. Maybe another guy joined because he felt like this was the only way to prove to himself he wasn't a coward.

Maybe the hero is teamed up with someone that is a complete opposite. The hero's a neat freak, the partner is a slob. The hero is highly-educated, but his right-hand man barely got his GED. Maybe one of the team members is a KKK sympathizer, and another one is black.

As with the opposition, the key here is taking a moment to ask what points of conflict the good guys might have with our hero and then explore the individual goals, motives, and plans behind those conflicts.

With Bit Characters and Other Intelligent Things

After looking at the main characters in the story who have goals and plans that conflict with the hero's, you might want to see if there are any bit characters who might provide points of conflict.

Maybe the hero drives into some bad neighborhood to try to get information from a witness. When the hero comes out from her meeting, she finds her car stolen.

Maybe in one scene the bad guys start shooting at a playground. The hero rushes them, but a mother who is trying to get her son off the swing thinks he's a bad guy, draws her weapon, and begins to shoot!

Maybe the hero needs to get into a building, but the guy working security has a mortgage in default and can't lose his job.

Maybe our hero is trying to get away and a vigilante truck driver hears the chatter over the police channel and decides to help.

Think about the other people that might in the scenes and what conflicts they might pose. If one is too delicious not to use it, put it in.

With Self

When the hero has two mutually exclusive goals, that's called a dilemma. Dilemmas aren't necessary, but they are delicious.

Maybe, like Katniss in *Hunger Games*, the heroine wants to live, but in order to do that she has to kill a boy who has been nothing but kind to her family. She wants to survive and be kind. But she can't do both.

Maybe like John Proctor in *The Crucible* the hero can keep his honor, but only if he dies. He wants his honor. He wants to be a good man. He also wants to live. But he can't do both.

Maybe like Bob in *The Incredibles*, the hero wants to escape a life of drudgery, but he also wants to keep his family safe. Alas, he can't have both.

You can present dilemmas at the beginning, middle, or end of a story.

One common dilemma brings the hero to a moment of choice at the climax. He can either do the wrong thing and survive. Or he can do the right thing and lose horribly. For example, the sheriff in a Western might come to the climax where it looks like certain death if he walks into the town. He's outmanned and outgunned. There appears to be no way he can win the fight. But if he walks away, he will leave the townspeople in the hands of those criminals.

Another type of dilemma isn't between right or wrong, but between two rights. For example, the hero wants to save the love of his life, but he also wants to save the village, and he can't do both. Or maybe the hero wants to enjoy her wonderful family. But there's some dark creature on the loose, and she's the only one with the powers to hunt it. If she goes hunting, there's a big chance she might die. Does she want to sacrifice being with her family for this? This could be a dilemma that's presented at the beginning of the story. The point is that it's hard to solve a problem when doing so means you must give up something else of great worth.

Another type of dilemma is a reverse temptation. Temptation presents you with something delicious in the short-term that's detrimental in the long term. A diet of doughnuts and milk, a romantic affair, and the high of heroin all feel great in the short term. In the long term they don't. The reverse temptation flips this. It's something we see a lot of in romance stories. A woman will meet a man, but she immediately convinces herself that falling in love with him will be a bad thing. It's going to cause all sorts of problems. The whole story, then, is about her coming to the realization that it won't be bad, but terrific. Instead of fighting temptation, she's fighting the good thing.

When developing your story, take some time to explore potential conflicts inside the main character. You don't have to include these types of conflicts in every story, but when you come up with a good one, it's such a lovely way to put your hero and readers through the wringer.

BAD LUCK AND TROUBLE

Life happens. The car's battery dies. The hero sprains an ankle. A fog rolls in. When things go wrong, it can cause our heroes a lot of wonderful trouble.

The setting can often be a great source of these types of issues. This includes the geography, weather, technology, culture, religion, government, tools, cars, buildings, elevators, squeaky shoes that give our hero away, etc.

So maybe the hero needs to cross a mountain range, but it just snowed, and it's deep.

Or the hero needs to steal a boat, but the tide moved the boat to a spot that will expose the hero to the guards on the beach.

Or the hero needs to get into a building, but the doors are locked.

Or the hero needs to speed away, but he can't get the car to go over thirty miles per hour because the car's a piece of junk.

Or something or someone from his past shows up to cause problems.

Machines break. Tools can be ornery. A sandstorm can mess up almost anything.

Maybe the hero wants to stop the two men who have kidnapped his little boy, but there's a river raging between him and them.

Maybe the hero has to hike twenty miles to the pickup point, but the temperature drops and drops and drops until it's fifty below and he only has minutes to live.

Maybe the hero encounters asteroids, trains that are late, horses that are high-spirited, and insects with wicked bites.

Maybe a hurricane is coming in and making it rough for our brave gal to go out to sea to save her husband whose boat is swamped.

Look around in your setting and see what unexpected obstacles might make it harder for the character, what things might not work as hoped, or how plans might go awry.

SURPRISE

Surprise is a magical ingredient in stories. When you twist your characters, THOMs, and obstacles in a surprising way, it can make your story so much more interesting.

Let's say you have a story about an assassin who needs to go behind enemy lines. Let's try twisting the conflict a bit so it's not just kill the bad guy. What if our character isn't just going in to get some random bad guy, but has been asked to sneak in and kill her sister? Or her mother? Or her best friend? Or maybe the person she needs to kill isn't in enemy territory but is a beloved religious leader or someone in our own government?

Let's give our hero a surprising twist. What if our assassin is not an adult CIA operative, but a child who has been trained for such work? Or maybe she's a grandmother with no training at all who is forced into the situation.

Can you feel how the unexpected piques your interest? And all you need to do is twist the elements of the setup with options that aren't what we normally expect.

You might think that your surprise won't be surprising enough. That's possible, but you'd be surprised how little surprise you need. This is because our miracle brains focus on the concrete surface details of a situation. That's why we can enjoy mystery after mystery, romance after romance, epic fantasy after epic fantasy, thriller after thriller when they all follow the same general pattern. The particulars of the stories are different enough. So while the situation may be similar, it's not the exact same thing readers have seen before, and so it prevents them from predicting how things will unfold. It's the same, but different. While the readers suspect what might happen, then don't know what will happen. And that allows us to deliver yet another awesome ride.

Another way to surprise readers is with misdirection. We purposely lead them to expect one thing, then reveal something else. Sometimes you do that by structuring the story so the lead character, and the reader, don't have all the facts up front. And the current set of facts lead to one conclusion. Sometimes you skillfully plant ideas into the reader's mind that misdirect their expectations. A classic example of this is the red herring in mysteries. But you can use it in other ways. For example, you can introduce a sidekick that the reader trusts. Only later do you reveal the sidekick is a traitor.

Another way to use surprise is by making sure things do not work as the hero plans. So the heroine in a romance decides that she can't pretend to be married to move star anymore and goes to tell him. But when she arrives, his five-year-old daughter who has fallen in love with our heroine is there, and our character can't drop the bomb.

The key to all of this is knowing what your reader is likely to be expecting and to then do something else. Or at least try something else.

Sometimes the expected thing is the awesome thing. Not everything has to be surprising.

One last note. Surprises must be believable to work. They need to be logical. Readers will not hope or fear if the opportunity or threat is hokey or forced. Rubber snakes only scare people when they're mistaken for the real thing. So give the audience surprises that make sense and watch their tension and delight rise.

INCREASING DIFFICULTIES

Another way to make a problem harder to solve is by making it grow in difficulty despite, or because of, the character's actions. This doesn't mean the characters can't solve small parts of the problem along the way. It doesn't mean good things can't happen to the character during the course of the story. After all, we want to fear and *hope* for the characters. And so we want some hopeful moments.

For example, in the middle of *The Hunger Games*, we get two nice chapters where things are looking up for Katniss. Of course, we don't want to think about the fact that she's going to have to eventually kill the person she's teamed up with. Or the fact that the careers are out there killing off everyone else, narrowing down the contestants until there will be nobody else but Katniss to hunt. So Katniss still has problems, but for a few chapters we get a break from the tension. And then we're plunged back in, worse than before.

Yes, we want small successes. But despite the successes, we want the tension in our readers to build, which means we need to make the difficulties worse.

How does this happen?

As our character attempts to solve the problem, she will experience disasters, calamities, setbacks, misfortunes, upsets, betrayals, unforeseen obstacles, desertions, and failures. Plans will go awry. The villain will counter with shocking blows. The character will learn things that twist her (and the reader's) understanding of the problem in more dangerous directions. The problem will become more intense, more immediate, probable, significant, and specific. More in the character's life will be put at risk.

Maybe the character starts the story being personally threatened by the villain, but as the story progresses, the villain begins to threaten the hero's children. Maybe our inexperienced team sets out, and halfway through the story the star player on their team, think of Gandalf or Obi-wan Kenobi, is killed. Maybe our airplane gets shot and the fuel leaks out, and our perfect escape crashes into the mountains only miles from where we began.

All of these plot turns keep the tension building.

Another thing these complications do is keep the story from becoming monotonous. A fight where the positions of the hero and the opposition remain static quickly begins to bore. Think of a football game where the score remains at 0-0 for three and half quarters. Both sides keep getting the ball and keep having to punt after three downs. Nobody gets injured. Nobody makes any yardage. Nothing changes.

Boring.

So we keep the plot turning, adding complications and revelations, and conflicts and surprises. We keep giving the reader something new to increase their hopes or fears.

You will get into the details of plotting and progressing the story with a sequence of bigger and bigger obstacles in the course on creating outlines. But you can add surprise by doing some things that are unexpected with the characters, THOM, and obstacles.

WORST FEARS REALIZED

You don't really feel the drug-like relief of a tall glass of cold water until you're bone-thirsty, desert dry. You don't really feel the weeping gratitude for a warm house until you're on the point of frostbite, or maybe have already lost a toe. And you don't really feel the rush of triumph unless you thought all was lost.

For many genres, our readers want to feel triumph. You can help them feel that if you actually help them think all is lost before the climax. This allows our characters to snatch victory from the jaws of defeat.

Now, you don't have to develop a dark moment for the story setup, but there's no harm in thinking about it at this stage. In the class on outlines, you're going to learn how to create dark moments because readers love what dark moments allow them to feel later. But if you get an idea for one now, capture it. If not, don't sweat it.

To this point we've looked at characters, THOMs, and obstacles in detail. There are two more elements that can go into a story setup. Before we get to them, I want to talk about some things that frequently knock new writers out of the game. If you're not prepared, these tigers can send you packing.

10

DON'T TURN A GARDEN HOSE INTO A SNAKE

When I first moved my family to the hinterlands of Utah, we lived here.

Grandma Edna's place

It was a nine hundred square foot house that my wife's grandmother had homesteaded for. It was made from logs that were later covered with white siding. It had a sloped floor (great for baking cakes when you wanted one side thicker than the other); a free-standing, fire-burning stove in the kitchen; and one bathroom next to the kitchen sink with a trick door that would pop open at random times so you could say hello to the folks while sitting on the toilet.

In the fall, you could hear the elk bugling at night. In the winter, you could stand on a hill, howl, and have one of the three packs of coyotes that lived in the valley bark and howl back at you. And year round you could frequently hear the calls of the multitude of peacocks a neighbor across the valley kept.

It was remote.

I worked in that little souped-up cow shed you see in the back. One summer day I took a break and walked to the house. Just as I got to the corner, I stepped on something black snaking through the grass.

I immediately jerked back. A surge of adrenaline hit. My heart began to palpitate. Holy mackerel! A snake!

And then I saw the snake extended fifteen feet away, and my brain said, whoa, wait a minute. A 15-foot long snake?

It wasn't a snake. It was actually a black garden hose.

I relaxed, my heart started to slow, and I laughed and went inside.

What this story illustrates is that we can appraise a situation in a completely distorted way. And authors are particularly prone to a number of distortions that sap their ability to produce and lead to all sorts of unnecessary fears, blocks, doubts, and discouragement.

Half of writing, it seems, is a head game. Let's make sure you see things clearly so you're not turning the garden hoses of writing into snakes.

SITUATION 1: YOU JUST READ SOMEONE ELSE'S STORY THAT'S AMAZING

Sometimes writers will read someone else's work and suddenly think, "Man, I can't do that. I'll never be that good. I can't come up with those kinds of ideas. How can I compete? I should just give up."

That right there is one big snake appraisal of the situation.

A more realistic view would actually be: "They did an awesome job. I have had some cool ideas. I might not be able to do what they do yet, but I bet I can learn. What were they doing that worked so well?"

Here are the actual truths about the situation.

Truth 1: Someone will always be better at writing than I am. That's normal.

Writing is a complex cognitive skill. That's one of the things that makes it so wonderful—we'll never get bored because there's so much to learn. In fact, we'll never learn it all and master every technique and type of story before we die. And because there is so much to learn, someone will always be better at some aspect of it than you are. Always. Even when you're a bestseller.

Truth 2: The problem with comparing myself to another author is that it's almost always apples to oranges.

You have no idea how long the other author has been writing.

You don't know how many books they've read, and therefore the material they have at their fingertips. I have a friend who read over two hundred romances before she started writing romances. Do you think she had insights that those who had only read a dozen or two didn't? It's not a fair comparison.

You don't know if that writer suddenly stumbled onto an insight because they happened to go to some conference or pick up some book.

You don't know if that writer had gobs more time to write or a stellar teacher along the way or dozens of other things.

Most importantly, none of that matters. You are where you are on the writing path. Regardless of where you are and how old you were when you started, you can progress along the path. You can read those two hundred romance novels, you can get the insights, you can improve your craft. Humans are learning machines. And you can learn it. And soon enough you'll be the one with the story that makes another author swoon.

Truth 3: We often learn by seeing what others do well. Their success is actually a gift.

All of us get blown away by how another author did something. At that moment we should rejoice because we now have an opportunity to see what they did. And monkey see monkey adapt it.

If someone else writes a terrific book, feel a bit of professional jealousy, and then figure out what they did.

SITUATION 2: YOUR STORY FEELS STUPID

Something will happen and you'll begin to say, "This is so dumb. No way can it compete. It has to be awesome. I should be able to do this. Why can't I get good ideas? Maybe I just don't have what it takes."

A more accurate statement would be: "It's not reasonable to expect a final product when you start. Pixar doesn't. They and other great story tellers often start with something that's only so-so and improve it."

Here are the truths about this situation.

Truth 1: Creativity flourishes when you value crap like farmers do.

We've already explored this.

Truth 2: Something is better than nothing. It's always easier to improve something than to start with a blank slate. So get something down quickly.

Louis L'Amour put it this way.

> "Start writing, no matter about what. The water does not flow until the faucet is turned on. You can sit and look at a page for a long time and nothing will happen. Start writing and it will."

Truth 3: It is not reasonable to expect a finished product at the beginning of the process. It is reasonable to expect a mess that gets better.

We all want things to be great right from the start. But novels are big projects, and there will sometimes be a period of time when the story, scene, beginning, ending, dialogue exchange, etc. isn't yet where you want it to be. That's fine. Write it down. Once you do, it becomes so much easier to see where to take it from there.

SITUATION 3: YOU STARTED AT THE SAME TIME AS SOMEONE ELSE, AND THEY'RE HAVING MORE SUCCESS

Sometimes you'll see another author having more commercial success than you are. And the kicker is they started writing at the same time you did or even much later.

You might be led to appraise the situation as a snake. "I should be better than they are. What's wrong with me? Maybe I don't have what it takes."

A more reasonable view is that "Much of commercial success is beyond my control. And I don't know where she started, how hard she worked, or what factors came into play. I just need to look at how far I've come. As long as I keep writing and learning, I'll get better."

Here are the truths about this situation.

Truth 1: Not everyone gets the same opportunities. The best thing I can do is work hard and learn so I'm ready for those that come my way.

Brandon Sanderson was a midlist author when Robert Jordan, one of his literary heroes, died. Jordan's wife tapped Sanderson to finish the series. Sanderson worked his guts out and finished the series brilliantly. Because of that, his career took off. But what would have happened if Sanderson hadn't gotten that mega chance? And how many Robert Jordans are out there who die with unfinished series?

The son-in-law of one of my neighbors just happened to be the book buyer for Kroger foods. This is back in 2009 when grocery stores had decent-sized book sections. At the time Barnes and Noble had something like 700 stores. Kroger had thousands, which gave an author much more exposure.

Well, my neighbor, without any prompting from me, talked to his son-in-law who told him to have me give him a call. I did. He told me the publisher hadn't mentioned my book. And why would they? I was just a baby author. But the buyer told me to send him the book. If they liked it, they'd put it in their stores in the western region of the United States.

They liked it. They put it in the stores in hardback. Some other grocery store book distributor saw what they were doing, and so when Kroger put it out in paperback, the other distributor put it in paperback in a bunch of non-Kroger stores as well.

That's a weird pigs-flying-on-brooms opportunity. And it would simply be unreasonable for another author to look at me being in so many grocery stores and conclude anything about their own writing or prospects.

Truth 2: Everyone progresses at their own pace and in their own way.

We all have different amounts of time we can spend on writing. We all have different times when we get our insights. We all start from different levels of storytelling. That's okay. The fact that someone is ahead of me in some way doesn't mean I'm not traveling down the road.

The better you understand the three things you need to know to write killer stories, the better your stories will be and the easier it will be to write them. So focus on learning those three things.

Truth 3: The odds for big commercial success are long. I can improve them with hard work and learning about the craft and business, but there are no guarantees how long it will take me.

Some people find success early. Some find it late. If you find it's taking too long to find success for your tastes, you may decide it's not worth the time. That's okay. Otherwise, continue increasing your skills in the three things you need to learn to write killer stories.

Truth 4: The problem with comparing myself to another author is that it's almost always apples to oranges.

We've seen this one before.

SITUATION 4: SOMEONE DOESN'T LIKE YOUR STORY

Some people won't like your story setup. Some beta readers won't like your story. Some customers who buy your books aren't going to like them. We might have 200 four- and five-star reviews, but then along comes one reader who gives it one star.

Writers often get tempted to appraise this as a snake. "How did I miss that issue? Why can't I do better? I'm not a very good writer like author Y. My writing stinks. I don't have what it takes."

A more realistic assessment is, "I have lots of good responses to my story. The story is working for many people. Is this person perhaps not in the audience for my book? I'm not in the audience for lots of books others love."

The truth about this situation is this: The audience for any book is only a small fraction of readers. It's okay if a person is not in my audience.

Remember this quote I shared with you before.

> "No matter who the writer, his ideal intended audience is only a small fraction of all the living readers. Name the most widely read authors you

can think of–from Shakespeare, Austen, and Dickens to Robert Waller, Stephen King, and J.K. Rowling–and the immense majority of book-buyers out there actively decline to read them" (Thomas McCormack)

SITUATION 5: A LOT OF PEOPLE DON'T LIKE YOUR STORY

What happens when a lot of people don't like the story and you get a significant number of negative responses?

When this happens, it seems almost impossible to not appraise it as a snake: "I'm a failure. Maybe I've lost it. Maybe all my successes were accidents and I never had what it takes."

A more realistic view is this: "Many of the best authors write a story that I don't like as well as their others. While I may have screwed up this performance, I can learn from it and do better. Also, some did like it."

Here are the truths about this situation.

Truth 1: It's just one performance. I can figure out what went wrong and fix it.

One bad performance doesn't mean you'll never have another good one. If that were true, every athlete would give up on sports before they made it out of middle school.

Truth 2: Many awesome authors have a dud now and then. That's what happens when you try new things.

Think about your favorite authors. Have they written a book you didn't like as much as the others? I'm betting they did. James Patterson, Stephen King, Nora Roberts, Bernard Cornwell, Dean Koontz, Tess Gerritsen—you fill in the blank. They are all terrific writers. And they have all written a book or two that just isn't as well-liked as others.

Truth 3: It's okay to feel down for a minute, then look to see what I can learn.

It's okay to feel disappointed about a performance that wasn't quite up to snuff. However, that's not the end. You have a miracle monkey brain. You can figure out what went wrong and learn from it.

Now there's one more situation that writers frequently view as a snake when it's just the opposite. In fact, it's so common it's got its own term. Let's discuss it so you can see it clearly and actually use it to supercharge your writing.

11

SPIDERMAN, PETER PARKER, AND THE GIFT OF WRITER'S BLOCK

Have you ever had this experience? You want to write a new story, but can't seem to get ideas. Or you've been going gangbusters and suddenly hit a snag, and you try and try, but just can't seem to make any progress.

"I always struggle," you might say. "I should be able to just flow right through the whole novel because that's what real authors do. Maybe I just don't have what it takes."

Folks, that's a snake. One of the biggest ones out there. But we can fix that appraisal with a little lesson from Peter Parker in *Spider-Man 2*.

In the movie, Peter starts off as Spider-Man.

He's got his cool outfit, a good-looking girlfriend who can hang on when he's pulling multiple gees, and crazy gravity-defying powers.

But then his powers start to fade, and Peter turns into a doofus. It gets so bad that in one scene Peter's climbing a wall when his spidey grip fails him, and he falls to the ground. He stands up, looking at his hands with a what-the-heck expression.

How could Spidey lose his superpowers?

He began losing them because he was trying to suppress his spidey-ness. He was trying to suppress who he was.

This is what writers do all the time. Instead of going out and

Create Story Ideas that Beg to be Written

swinging from the skyscrapers, they turn into creative doofuses because they deny their essential storyness and end up unable to wield any power at all.

What am I talking about?

I'm talking about writer's block.

Nooooooooo! The horror, the horror.

Okay, stop with the psycho music. Writer's block is not one of the bad guys. Writer's block is exactly the opposite. It's a gift.

Somehow, this truth was turned onto its head. And it causes problems wherever it goes. Writer's block is not something to be avoided. It can't be. Because it's a natural part of the process. "Writer's block" is really the fabulous inner spidey sense we have for story. And this inner story sense starts acting up when certain things begin to go wrong.

THE WRITER'S TRANCE

As I've pointed out, good ideas carry current, they spark your interest, they tug your heart strings, they turn you on. It's the feeling of "cool," "whoa," or "oh, boy, this has possibilities."

When the sparks combine in the right way, you slip into the writer's trance where the story just flows. Others call this the flow state or being in the zone. When in this mental state, you're constantly thinking to yourself: "Ah, yes, that's what he'd do," or, "Oh, man, yeah, this is what's got to happen now," or "Oh, baby, that's perfect." You can see the story roll out in front of you like a red carpet. And you write at speed. Whatever speed means for you.

But the fact is that while we may come up with a cool idea or six, start the story with a bang, move to the next scene or chapter (or even to the end), at some point something suddenly pulls the plug, and everything grinds to a halt.

I used to go into the throes of woe when this happened because I took this to mean I wasn't a real writer. It meant I didn't have writer genes. I didn't have the writer's personality type. Good grief, I sometimes thought it meant God did not want me to write.

Drama, drama, drama.

All that angst was rubbish. That fact is that the trance comes and goes. For everybody. End of story. Don't expect your process to work any differently. I don't know any author who doesn't experience this when writing a large project like a novel. This means you should expect to run out of juice. You should expect parts to feel dull. You should expect to hit snags.

When the trance goes, it's not a sign from the heavens. It's a sign that something is off, and you just need to listen to it so you can get back on track.

Here are the main trance breakers and what each is telling you to do.

BREAKER 1: HEY, FEED YOUR BEAST

With this breaker, you'll notice you don't know what is supposed to happen next or what the characters are supposed to say or do. You literally don't know what to write.

Here's the diagnosis and fix. You've simply written to the end of your invention. The fridge and cupboards are bare. Determine what story element you need next, go hunt down some zing to feed your beast, follow the creative principles, and start generating options.

If you need to, take a walk. I take creative walks all the time. As I said before, I staple two pieces of paper together, get a pencil, and then head outdoors and talk to myself, generating options as I go. One particular issue took me about twelve miles over three days walking up a canyon by our house to finally get the solution that carried the zing. Sooner or later, you'll have a zing storm, and the trance will return.

BREAKER 2: HEY, YOU FORGOT TO FOLLOW THE RULE OF COOL

With this breaker, you'll notice your story bores you. Instead of feeling excited or drawn to the story, you have to push yourself to write. This is not the same as not knowing what to write next. You know what comes next, but it's lifeless and boring. It tastes like bland oatmeal.

Here's the diagnosis and fix. You've developed something lacking zing. Well, big hairy deal. Something is better than nothing. What you need to do now is find the zing trail again. Review the things that make characters, THOMs, plots, settings, etc. interesting and identify what you think your story lacks. Then follow the creative principles, and start generating options.

BREAKER 3: HEY, YOU KNOW THAT DOESN'T MAKE SENSE

With this breaker, you'll notice it feels made up. You recognize things wouldn't work that way. Or you recognize what you want the character to do isn't what they'd naturally do in that situation.

Here's the diagnosis and fix. You've developed something that doesn't ring true. Another big whoop. Identify what it is that doesn't ring true, follow the creative principles, and start generating options that would make sense.

BREAKER 4: HEY, STOP COMPARING YOURSELF

With this breaker, you'll notice you keep feeling it's not good enough, not original enough. It's not going to blow the competition away. You can't compete. Why should you even write when books like the one you just read exist?

Here's the diagnosis and fix. You've fallen into the comparison trap. You don't have to please every reader on the planet. You don't have to sell millions of copies. You don't have to be as good as someone else because there will always be someone better than you. And your story doesn't have to be perfect. You don't think so? Take a hard look at some of your favorite books. Is every chapter equally enthralling? Every character equally delightful? Ask the authors if there aren't things they'd go back and change. So just chill. Quit trying to impress everyone. Just tell a story that jazzes you and that your kids or brother or sister would like.

BREAKER 5: HEY, BREAK THE PROJECT DOWN INTO SMALLER STEPS

With this breaker, you'll think, holy crap, I can never do this! It's too big. Too difficult. It's going to take a billion years, and it just exhausts me thinking about where to begin.

Here's the diagnosis and fix. You've forgotten that novels are big projects. And they're even bigger for folks who haven't done one before. But folks complete big projects all the time. A little bit each day adds up. Mary Higgins Clark wrote a little each day and became a huge bestseller. So have many others. And even if what you produce today is crap, that's fine. It's progress. Something is always better than nothing. The story you have on paper is always more valuable to you than the one you have in your head.

What you need to do is break down what you have to do into major steps and the sub-tasks for each step. You want these tasks to be small enough that you can complete them in a writing session or three. A task list is incredibly helpful.

Let me share with you the main steps in my novel projects. Use them until you find your own.

Novel Project Steps

1. Develop High-interest Ideas

- Create a story setup that begs to be written
- Create an outline of story that keeps readers on the edge of their seat

2. Write Chapters That Transport the Reader

- Write first draft
- Print and edit first draft
- Update for edits (second draft)
- Send to beta readers
- Update for responses (third draft)
- Get copy edit
- Update for edit (final draft)

3. Publish Attractive Product

- Get cover made (although I sometimes start it earlier)
- Format and proofread

- Write description, including tag line
- Publish

4. Market Intelligently

Identify where you are in this process. Don't worry about the later steps until you get to them. Once you know which step you're on, identify some of the tasks you know you need to finish for that step. When you've done that, circle the three you think are most important. Then start to work on them.

You don't need to write every possible task out in the beginning. Just write out the project steps. Identify the tasks of the current step that you see clearly right now. And get to work. As you work on the current tasks for a given step, others will present themselves, and you can add them to your list. When you finish a step, celebrate.

Finally, if you really want to keep moving, take one minute at the end of every writing session to jot down the simple task you want to accomplish in the next session.

BREAKER 6: HEY, GO GET SOME SLEEP

With this breaker, you'll notice you can't stay awake. You bonk your head on the keyboard or suddenly jerk awake. You can barely think.

Here's the diagnosis and fix. This isn't a hard one—go take a nap. Or just go to bed. If it happens all the time, work on your sleeping habits.

BREAKER 7: "HEY, GET YOUR OVEN HOT"

With this breaker, you know you have created a lot of good stuff. You know you felt lots of zing, but, heck, it's not really there now. You feel like you're always reviewing your old notes to remember what you'd sketched and planned.

Here's the diagnosis and fix. You are not spending enough time on the project, and so you're spending all your time trying to remember what you developed before. If you haven't worked on a project for a while, it *will* go cold. The fix is to spend consistent time focused on the project.

However, don't think this means you need four-hour chunks of time. You can get up 30 minutes earlier in the morning to review the current scene you're writing. You can sketch what you want to write during your breaks. You might be able to write for 15-20 minutes during lunch. That way you're ready to dive in during your session later that night or the next morning. Working on your story in smaller chunks throughout the day can help keep your oven hot.

EMBRACE THE TRUTH

You might get other signals from your story sense. The point is to remember that the trance will come and go. When it goes, that doesn't mean you're a story moron. It means your story sense is telling you something. Stop and listen. Identify what it's telling you and take the appropriate action.

When you do, the lights will eventually turn back on, the music will begin to play, and the words will again roll off your fingertips...until the next break. Because that's just the way the process works. You're going to run into story snags. And then you're going to get unstuck, and the process will flow again.

Having alerted you to the head games writers need to be aware of, it's time to discuss the last few elements of the story setup. If you recall, one of the main elements of the setup was a compelling character. But you need more than one character. You need a cast. And there are some key things to remember when developing one. That's the topic of the next chapter.

12

INTERESTING CASTS

A wonderful cast will please your readers immensely. It can provide more humor, more tension, more secrets—more of everything. However, a poor cast can undermine your reader's enjoyment. Use the tips below to make sure your cast is working well.

 SPEND THE TIME EACH DESERVES

I find it useful to think about characters by how much stage time they'll have.

- **Major** characters get a lot of stage time because the story revolves around them.
- **Secondary** characters play a smaller role in helping and hindering the hero.
- **Bit** characters get hardly anytime at all. They have a function to perform, and then they need to get out of the way so we can keep the spotlight on the major characters. In fact, bit characters might not even get any lines.

When creating the story setup, my suggestion is to focus your development time on the main characters. You don't need to spend much if any time on the bit characters. Heck, I spend hardly any time on them at all. When I do get to them during the plot or writing of the chapters, I usually just exaggerate some characteristic that I think is fun and call it good.

2. THINK ABOUT THEIR ROLES

The other characters are there to help, hinder, or provide interesting dynamics.

Characters that help are those that have skills, knowledge, or a temperament that complement those the hero has. For example, if the hero is great at swords, maybe the sidekick is lousy with the sword, but is a terrific thief. Or maybe the hero is a newbie and would benefit from seasoned advice. That's the role of a mentor. Or maybe it would help the hero to have someone who has tons of physical brawn. Or someone who is a whiz at technology. Or is a doctor. Or maybe the hero is rash, and the sidekick is more level-headed and provides a good sounding board. Maybe the sidekick is the one to exercise hope when the hero feels all hope is gone. There are lots of things that might help your character. Let the other characters provide those things.

Characters that hinder the hero are those that help the antagonist. They work in the same way. So maybe the villain is shrewd and uses his brains. He might be helped by having someone tough who can perform physical violence. Or maybe the villain is physically imposing and hires a conniving accountant to help him. Or maybe he benefits from talking things over with someone who has a conniving brain.

Characters that hinder the hero might also be on the hero's team. Maybe the other person is from a tribe that's normally an enemy, but the two are paired up to defeat a common foe. Or maybe the other person is really there to help the hero only to a certain point, and then kill the hero or leave him in the ditch. Or maybe the person has great skills, but he drinks too much and can sometimes cause problems.

Finally, there are lots of characters who can provide fun and interesting dynamics. There might be a love interest, or someone from a social class that's totally different from another member of the team.

Create Story Ideas that Beg to be Written

Maybe one is quirky and another has a secret past. Maybe one provides the reader some comic relief. Or maybe two members of the cast approach things from a totally different angle: one is overly logical while the other is overly driven by emotions, or one is proper and reserved while the other is low brow.

You're looking for those that help, hinder, or provide some story fun.

3. LESS IS OFTEN MORE

Having too many main and secondary characters can ruin your story. At best it will clutter up the reader's experience. At its worst it will prevent you from developing any one character sufficiently.

You'd think that a single story of 25,000 to 100,000 words has plenty of room for lots of parts, but it doesn't. It seems that somewhere around four to six characters works well for a single story of that size. It gives each of character enough stage time to actually contribute.

For the good guys, you have the hero, a sidekick, or team of sidekicks. There might be a mentor. There might be a love interest. For the bad guys you have the antagonist. And there might be a henchman and an assortment of lackeys. Or there might be a team of henchmen.

My suggestion is to identify four to six folks from that crowd of good guys and bad guys that you want to focus on, and make all of the rest of them secondary characters. If you need to reduce, look for ways to combine characters so one person performs multiple roles, allowing you to drop the characters that are now superfluous from the tale.

I've also found that four to six main characters seem to be the max readers can keep straight in any individual scene. Let's just do some math. My average scene length is somewhere around 2,000-2,500 words.

If I have six major characters in a scene, that means each gets around 400 words. But even that's not accurate because I have to remove the word count for description. What if I double the number to twelve characters all vying for the spotlight? Now each gets less than 200 words.

With that number of people I also blow past the reader's working memory limits. Trying to stuff so many major parts into a scene makes it hard for a reader to even remember who is there, let alone what each one is like.

The same goes for heroes and antagonists. It's usually more powerful to have one villain instead of a hundred of them. One hero instead of fifteen. Having more just waters down the effect. Yes, the hero and villain will have helpers, but having one hero and one villain allows us to focus.

Of course different genres require different things. So look at a few of the books you love. Look at three to four scenes in each and count how many characters have speaking parts. Then identify how many have major parts in the scene. I think you'll find they have fewer than you think.

MAKE 'EM DIFFERENT

Finally, we need to make sure our cast is interesting as a group. And that means you need to make each one different. This is sometimes referred to as cast orchestration, as in you don't want an orchestra made up of nothing but kettle drums.

For example, let's say you have a team of characters who need to go behind enemy lines to find and dismantle a radar station. If every one of those team members is exactly the same—they're all big, blond football players from Oklahoma with the exact same personality type, we might find it funny and odd at first, but it will soon lose its appeal as they all say, do, and think the same things.

Compare this to a group where one is a thief from the inner city, another is a philosopher, another is a neat freak, a fourth is a short ladies' man, the last is a wise-cracking American Indian. Maybe one joined the Army because he's got first-person shooter games dancing in his eyes, another because his father was a military man, another is there to conduct some kind of criminal heist, the fourth because he's poor and needed help getting through college and supporting his wife and kid, and the last because it was his only way out of jail.

Did you ever wonder why boy bands have a variety of types—the serious one, the good one, the bad one, the cutie? It's because it broadens the appeal to a wider audience.

But it goes beyond that. Variety also helps us avoids boredom. Imagine eating a meal that's nothing but salmon, broccoli, fried okra, or even ice cream. Imagine that's all you ever eat. You may be a cheese-lover, but after twenty dishes of cheese, you will get sick of it. We like variety in our food, and we like variety in our characters.

And it doesn't end there. There's an even more important reason for giving your cast variety: it opens up possibility for more conflict, surprise, and story. Maybe one of the lead's team members loses courage. Maybe one of the bad guys is thinking about doing his boss in. With some variety, you can not only write about the main problem, but you also add in subplots—a love story or a redemption plot. And both can complicate the central problem.

As mentioned before, you can enrich a cast by having a couple of points of conflict between the folks on the same team. So maybe two people on the hero's team drive each other nuts. One's a slob, the other is a neat freak. One's rule-keeper, the other is a rule-breaker. One's a conspiracy theorist, the other is a data man. Maybe a mentor disagrees with the hero on some things and vice versa.

With the bad guys you can do the same thing. Maybe there's a disagreement between two henchmen. If you watched *The Lord of the Rings*, you saw this when one orc wanted to eat Merry's and Pippin's legs, but the leader wanted to keep the hobbits "unspoiled."

Variety adds interest. Develop your characters with an eye toward the effect of the cast as a whole.

13

COOL LOCATIONS

You're going to be developing the setting much more in the last two phases of your novel project where you outline the story and write your chapters. However, there's some fun work you can do now that can help you in those phases and with the setup itself.

It's important to note that in some stories and genres the setting plays a bigger role in reader enjoyment, and you will need to spend more time developing it. For example, a big part of the draw of historical fiction, science fiction, and fantasy is about being transported to a different place and time. However, not all stories provide that level of transport because the reader delights are focused on other things. And that's okay. There's no one best role for setting to play.

Still, I've found it helpful to ask these questions at this stage:

- What's cool?
- What could give the hero trouble?

The story has to take place somewhere. What would be a fun or cool place? Once you determine that, what could be fun or cool things about that place you can use as a backdrop for all the action? And what details are a bit unexpected?

Create Story Ideas that Beg to be Written

For example, I love Southern Utah, and when it was time to write the second action thriller in my Frank Shaw series, I decided to set it there. There was no other reason than I thought the action needed to take place somewhere remote, and I thought that area was cool. <u>Once I located the specific area, I began researching, looking for cool stuff, and found these beauties</u>:

- Motorized paragliding.
- Big horn sheep.
- Collared lizards.
- Flash floods.
- A police force that parks a patrol car on a main road and puts a dummy in it. A smart and funny way to keep the many tourists driving the right speed.
- A grocery store with a massive, Paul-Bunyan-sized shopping cart out front.
- Polygamists.
- Slot canyons.
- A Mars habitat research center where scientists simulate living on Mars.
- Illegal marijuana grows manned by criminals with guns.

I drove down and visited the place to refresh my memory of it. While driving around, I passed a home where one of the deputy sheriffs lived. I stopped, asked if he'd be willing to chat, interviewed him, and explored some more. The zing and unexpected details continued to come:

- The wind blows the sand there so you'll get a skiff of it on the porch or at the base of your door like northern climes get skiffs of snow.
- The local sheriff offers man tracking courses every summer.
- A German bakery owned by...Germans.
- The fact that a lot of the vacation homes were owned by folks outside the state.
- A rock shop outside a little town called Orderville.
- A house with all sorts of old cars parked in the yard.

- A million-dollar lodge I could adapt and make the villain's lair.
- The fact that there are large parts of the back country without cell service.
- A house in the middle of the city with chickens roosting on the fence.
- An old gentleman with cowboy hat and chaps riding a horse down the middle of a street one quiet evening.
- A number of mind-blowing vistas.

I didn't know how, or if, I'd use all of this stuff, but that didn't matter. I was gathering zing. I was feeding my imaginative beast. I was looking for salient and unexpected details. I hiked around, noted some specifics about what the place looked like and what I saw in that desert.

Settings are wonderful source of obstacles. And so as I was finding all this zing, I was also asking what in the setting might create an obstacle to my hero's goal.

Right off the bat I saw that having no cell service could cause troubles. Getting chased into a blind canyon could cause another. Flash floods seemed likely. I did a bit more research and found a guy who chases flash floods in the area. I contacted him and asked if I could chat with him a bit. He agreed, and I called and got all sorts of wonderful, unexpected details about how a flash flood in that country forms, what it sounds and smells like, and what the true dangers are.

When I was done, I had a number of pages of notes, some pictures, and videos. Some of that made it into the book. Some of it didn't. What it all did, however, is help make the story come alive in my mind so I could develop the outline and chapters, and then help it come alive in the reader's mind.

As with characters, you don't need to write a book about the place. Especially not at this point. In the story setup phase you just need a list of what's cool, what could cause the hero trouble, and enough information to create a broad-brush +1 sketch of the dominant impression of the place.

Please note that as you dig into the setting you will probably get ideas for the events in your story. This just demonstrates that the phases

Create Story Ideas that Beg to be Written

of your novel project overlap. So if you get ideas for events and where those things might take place, note it. You'll do a lot more fleshing out of the various location when you outline and then write, but there's no reason not to note the dominant impression of a place in your setting sketch.

Again, the goal in this phase is not to discover everything you need to know about the setting as you write. You'll develop a lot of the setting when you sketch your outline and write your chapters. At this point, you're not trying to write an encyclopedia about the place. You're just trying to gather a bunch of zing, identify unexpected details, and have the place come alive in your mind.

For those of you writing science fiction or fantasy, you don't need to simply learn about a time and place, you have to invent it. So you're going to be spending a bit more time developing your setting. Please see the appendix for some tips on magic, creatures, cultures, etc.

Once you have your setting sketch, you need to consider one more thing for your setup. And we'll discuss that in the next chapter.

14

MULTIPLE STORYLINES

Your novel can include one storyline, or it can include multiple storylines. I'm not talking about one story told from the point-of-view of multiple characters. I'm talking about multiple stories, each with its own story setup, development, and conclusion.

A/B/C STORIES

A frequent combination is to tell an A and a B story. The A story is the main story and takes up a larger portion of the stage time. The B story deals with a smaller matter and takes up less of the stage time.

For example, the A story in a thriller might focus on the villain wanting to bomb the White House, and the B story would focus on the romance between the main character and the guy she's teamed up with. If you're writing a romance, you'd switch it. The A story would focus on the romance, and the B story would focus on dealing with the villain.

You can expand the number of storylines to include an A, B, and C (or more) stories. In this approach, the A story still takes up most of the time. The B story takes up less. The C story even less. You can use a 3:2:1 proportion where the A story takes up half the time, the B story a third, and the C story the rest. Or you can use some other proportion. Don't fall into the trap of thinking there's one right proportion.

If we add a C story to our thriller above, it might tell the story of a romance between a sidekick and someone else. Or it could focus on the hero reconciling with her mother. Or it might be a buddy story between two people on the hero's team. Or it could be about taking out some minor thug. Or it could be about an overarching plot that spans multiple books.

If you want to have more than three storylines, you can. You can have an A, B, C, D structure. Or an A, B, C, D, E, F, etc. one. What you have to realize is that (1) the more you have, the more complicated it makes the project for you, and (2) you only have so much stage time. Add too many storylines, and you limit the size of each story. Instead of giving the reader the feel of a big ride, you'll give them smaller rides. But if that's what you love, then do it.

What's the perfect number of storylines? There isn't one. The perfect number is the one that you can handle as a writer and delivers the experience you and your target audience loves most. However, I will say that if you're just starting out as a writer the most important thing you need to learn is how to develop and finish longer stories. The more of those you can finish, the faster you'll learn the craft. You might learn best by writing some of those simpler novels first and leaving the saga with fifty main characters and dozens of plots for later.

A/A/A STORIES

To this point we've been talking about a main storyline and subordinate storylines, sometimes called sub-plots. What if you want them to be equal? So instead of an A/B/C structure, you want an A/A or A/A/A structure where all the stories get the same amount of stage time?

For example, an A/A/A might be the stories of three different characters caught up in the same medieval war. One story focuses on the prince as he leads his armies. The second story follows an adolescent thief who was impressed into service. The third might be from the point of view of a female who has to fight off bandits who want rob and take advantage of the women who were left behind by their soldier husbands. The stories can affect each other as they go along or they can run parallel and meet up at the end.

When you tell A/A or A/A/A stories, you need to know that you run the risk of uneven interest, which occurs when your reader really likes the one story and is bored with the others. It's easier to avoid that risk if the stories affect each other.

How many A stories can you have?

Hopefully, you know my answer at this point—there isn't a right answer. It all depends on the experience you want to provide. Form follows function. However, if you want an extreme example, one of the most successful books I've read that pushes this A/A/A structure to the max is *World War Z* by Max Brooks. The book relates the story of the zombie war, but it does it through a series of oral interviews, which are really just first-person stories. There are fifty-seven interviews total from forty-two survivors. That's forty-two A stories. What Brooks does is group the interviews by stage of the war from the early warnings, the outbreak, apocalypse, conclusion, and aftermath. They all revolve around the war and help you see its progress.

Of course, they're all small stories. They can't give you the deep experience you can get by spending all that stage time with a handful of characters and one story problem. That's not better or worse; it's just a different type of experience.

By the way, Brooks got the idea for his approach from *The Good War* by Studs Terkel, a non-fiction collection of oral histories from soldiers in World War 2. It's a classic illustration of monkey see monkey adapt.

So how many storylines should you include? I'd recommend the number you can handle and enjoy the most.

SERIES

The final thing you will want to consider at this stage is whether your novel is part of a series. Series can be made up of two types of episodes:

- Stand-alone (also called episodic)
- Sequential (also called serial)

Create Story Ideas that Beg to be Written

The series of stand-alones is made up of stand-alone novels. You don't have to read them in any order. Each story may include one or more storylines, but they are all wrapped up in that single book.

You see this a lot with thrillers that feature a certain hero or mysteries that feature a special detective. Sherlock Holmes, Nancy Drew, Jack Reacher, Mitch Rapp, Monk, etc. Bernard Cornwell's Last Kingdom series does this by featuring its main character in a number of different Medieval, English battles.

But you don't always have to use the same character. There are many series that feature different characters in each book that are all in the same themed situation. For example, L.L. Muir has a huge series with over fifty books in it now, and each book is about a time travel romance that features a different Scotsman at the Battle of Culloden. Liz Isaacson wrote a Three Rivers Ranch series, and each book features a romance with different characters in a certain town.

Unlike the stand-alone series, the sequential series is made up of novels that build on each other. You'll often see this referred to as a "serial." Whichever word you use, the point is that you need to read them in order to know what's going on and enjoy them. For example, J.K. Rowling's Harry Potter series builds this way. As does J.R.R. Tolkien's *Lord of the Rings*.

In some serials the overarching plot takes the center stage in every book. In other series it might be the A story in one book, but in the next books it might be the C or D story. In other series, it can be a D story in the beginning and rise to the A story by the end of the series.

Finally, you can also have multiple B, C, and D story lines that span multiple books. Or you can finish each B, C, or D story in the book where it started. As you can see, there are a lot of different combinations of storylines that can please readers.

My three bits of advice if you're writing a sequential series are these. First, do not feel like you must know everything that's going to happen up front. For right now remember you're just doing the story setup; you're not outlining. So identify which stories will be resolved in the current novel, which will span multiple novels, and which one is the overarching plot.

Second, you'll probably find that more of your readers will like your serial novels when each novel gives them a sense of progression. That means each novel has a big story question that's raised in the beginning of the novel and is resolved at the end of that same novel. That story problem might focus on a step in the overarching plot. Or it might be its own story with the overarching plot playing a B, C, or D role.

When talking about a lack of progression, I'm not talking about a cliffhanger or tease at the end of a novel to propel readers forward to the next one. You can finish a satisfying story and immediately open another story that makes the reader want to go to the next book. What I'm talking about avoiding is asking your audience to read forty-, seventy-, or a hundred-thousand words, come to the end of it, and find that nothing is resolved. No progress has been made. You and your audience might be different, but I'm betting you're not. I'm betting you and your readers want to have an interesting story question triggered, delayed, and then delivered in the same book.

Finally, even if you want tons of storylines spanning multiple novels, don't feel like you have to write huge books that are three-hundred-thousand words long. You can write your big, rich, long story in installments as small as thirty-thousand words. If TV teaches us anything, it's that big stories can be told in small chunks. It satisfies the reader. It's easier for the writer. And it can be more profitable. When developing your series, think about how you might break it up. The TV approach might be exactly what you want.

If you think you want to write a series, take some time to think about whether you want it to be made up of stand-alone novels or whether you want them to be sequential. Series with stand-alones allow readers multiple entry points, so any of the books can snag the reader and lead them to read all the others. But you may have a big story to tell. And some authors and readers love, love, love the long story.

15

TWO EXPANDED STORY SETUPS

To this point, the book has focused on the elements of the story setup. In this chapter I want to present examples of full-blown setups so you can see what they're like. The idea here is simply to see how you can capture each element.

There are seven parts to a full story setup. The core elements include:

- Genre
- Compelling Character
- **THOM**
- Concrete goal
- Formidable obstacle

If it helps, use GC THOM GO to remember them. Then add the final two:

- Cast
- Setting

The genre focuses you on the salient aspects of the type of story and experience you want to develop. The character, THOM, goal, and obstacle capture the heart of the story. The cast captures who else will be part of the ride and whether they help or hinder. And the setting tells you where it will take place. In all of this we're following the rule of cool.

Both of the story setups below capture those things. However, before presenting them I want to make sure you don't fall into a form-over-function trap.

The goal of writing the story setup is not to follow the format I use below. The goal is not to describe characters, THOMs, or obstacles the way I describe them. Or to develop the elements in the order shown.

The goal is simply to summarize the key elements of your story in a way that helps you focus on what matters the most and brings it alive in your mind. So if pictures help you, use them. If they don't, forget them. If writing in paragraphs helps you, use them. If you prefer bullets, do that. You aren't writing the setup for anyone but yourself. Do what works for you. Keep the goal of the story setup in mind and use whatever helps you achieve that goal.

Remember: the purpose of the story setup isn't to nail down everything you need to know about the story. The purpose is to help you develop and capture the critical things you need in order to move to the next stage of development and begin imagining the plot.

Once you have the elements before you and feel the electricity of the tale, you have everything you need to outline a story that keeps readers on the edges of their seats (or to start writing chapters if you like to proceed by the seat of your pants).

STORY SETUP 1: BORDER LOVE

Let's take a look at the key elements of this story.

Genre

Clean, contemporary romance. The experience needs to have a happily-ever-after ending, lots of banter, some humor, a hero the readers can fall in love with, an admirable heroine, a dark moment, and opportunities to touch as the attraction and romance grows.

Create Story Ideas that Beg to be Written

Characters

I see four main characters for this story.

Camila Carrillo aka "Sweats"

Deputy Anna Murillo with some weed

Deputy Anna Murillo, Broward County, Florida

I'm using these pictures of the real-life police woman Anna Murillo in Broward County, Florida as inspiration. I came across them as I was doing research on police women for my thriller *Awful Intent*.

Camila lives in Texas and is a fun-loving border patrol agent who can take care of business. She's seen it all, from smugglers (coyotes) bringing girls across the border for sex slavery, to narcos working for Mexican drug cartels, to Asians wanting a better life, to little grannies wanting to just see their babies in El Norte. When off-duty, Camila prefers to fly under the radar. And so when asked about her work, she simply says she has a government job with too much paperwork.

Camila's divorced and has a five-year-old daughter named Carly. When Camila's at work, Carly stays with Mamita, Camila's abuelita (grandmother). Camila's mother lives in California, so she's out of the picture. Camila's ex-husband is a bit slimy, runs a successful company, drives glitzy cars, and frequently tells Camila she should come back and be his carina.

Camila's abuelita is always after her to get a man, but Camila is jaded. She doesn't have much time as a single mom, but she does love four-wheeling and the killer sweet rolls a local cafe makes every Wednesday.

Justin Wall

Justin is a single, happy-go-lucky Texan house builder with a big pickup truck who enjoys working outdoors and providing quality work. He learned how to sky dive when he was in the military and currently works as a sky diving instructor on the weekends at his buddy's business. He's also a coyote, helping families who have already crossed the United States border. The reason he's helping is because a few years ago he was working with a friend in Central America when a family was gunned down in front of him. He held the little girl as she bled out. At that moment he was compelled to do something. He wants to change government policy, but won't wait for that to help families in danger get to safety.

Mamita
A forceful granny who loves life and sometimes can be seen wearing white slacks with flames around the cuffs.

Carly
A cute five-year-old who loves fairy princesses who ride Tyrannosaurus Rexes.

Others

- Camila's ex. A bit slimy with glitzy cars.
- Camila's superior. No nonsense, super-experienced.
- Justin's female partner in his coyote activities. Married. An accountant for a manufacturing company.

Will there be more? Probably. Almost always more people show up when I outline and write the chapters. But this is who I see now.

THOM and Goal

Mamita has always wanted to learn how to skydive, and she tells Camila this is what she wants for her birthday. Despite the fact that Camila has a fear of heights, Camila purchases lessons for her and Mamita at the local skydiving club. Mamita selects the tall, strong instructor with the attractive scruffy look whose name is Justin. And Camila doesn't know what's worse—Mamita's obvious efforts at matchmaking, thinking about going up in the plane, or the feelings Camila gets when the instructor puts his arms around her.

Camila bought a package with a number of lessons. This ensures a reason for her and Justin to keep seeing each other. Also, Mamita will connive to get Justin to come around to the house to fix something for her, eat dinner, maybe do something else. She can see he's a good man, even if Camila won't open her eyes. Carly too will fall in love with him when he fixes her bike and helps her learn how to ride.

This is <u>a story of opportunity</u>. <u>So the reader is going to be wanting the two to get together and needs to hope and fear they won't</u>. Camila's goal will be to initially fight the growing attraction for reasons discussed below.

Obstacle

The first is obvious—she's a border patrol agent, he's a coyote, and both feel they're doing what's right. Also, Camila is a bit jaded and cautious, knowing people aren't always what they seem. In fact, as the relationship grows, she'll investigate him just to make sure, running background checks, etc. So even though the romance is going to progress, she'll be trying to find things to prove he's too good to be true. And then when she finally decides to go with the love she and her daughter feel for him, she'll find out what he does.

On Justin's side, I think he might learn earlier that she's Border Patrol. I think he might try to convince her to see another side and struggle with his feelings for her versus the people he's helping. I also have a feeling Camila's ex might cause some bad criminal elements to come after Justin later in the story.

How is all this going to work out and lead to a happily ever after? At this point, I have no idea. Figuring that out is part of the fun of the first draft, which can be an outline or actual chapters.

Locations

I'm thinking it will be set in San Angelo, the oasis of west Texas. There is a Border Patrol station there. And of the areas I looked at, it has some things I thought might be fun to feature in the story:

- The spectacular Big Bend National Park a few hours away.
- The three lakes and the Concho River around San Angelo.
- Concho pearls—beautiful natural freshwater pearls found inside the opalescent Tampico mussel shells at the bottom of rivers and lakes near San Angelo, Texas.
- Wild hog hunting at night.
- The Goodfellow Air Force base.

- Supposedly breathtaking sunsets and night skies. Good for romance.
- Bats. 100,000 plus bats swarm out from under the Foster Road overpass every night.
- San Angelo rodeo.
- The historic downtown.
- The skydiving plane, airport, etc.

I'll develop the location more when I get to the actual outline.

Setup Brief

- In this contemporary romance
- Camila is a late-twenties, divorced border patrol agent who prides herself on being able to catch and takedown anyone. She has a little girl who is the light of her life and a grandmother who is always conniving for Camila to get a man. But after the divorce Camila has become jaded about relationships with men.
- Justin is a single Texan who builds houses and teaches skydiving.
- When Justin becomes Camila's skydiving coach, Camila begins to maybe reconsider her feelings toward men.
- But will she be able to find true love
- When she discovers that Justin is not only a coyote, but the #1 smuggler she and her team have been hunting?

Note

I think the idea for a Border Patrol agent came from a mix of a news articles about illegal crossings and then me seeing the real-life officer Murillo holding that marijuana plant. I thought a great romance would be between her and a guy who just happened to be a coyote—the enemies trope thing. So I started this one with a picture for a character, went to THOM, and then bounced around, adding to and changing the elements of the setup as I went.

I originally imagined the book starting with Camila and team trying to interdict a group of those making an illegal crossing at night. A group that happened to be led by Justin. Of course, he'd get away. Later they'd meet in a cafe with killer sweet rolls. Maybe she'd be reading something about plumbing to fix a broken sink for Mamita, and he'd talk to her about it and give her advice. Then he'd offer to come and look at it.

I put the idea in my zing file a number of years ago. However, when I pulled the idea out and decided to use it for this course, I quickly realized it had a problem. Romances require the two characters to spend time together, and I didn't like the plumbing angle. That meant I didn't have anything but desserts on Wednesdays. I needed something better than that. I suppose you could write a romance called Sweet Wednesdays and have it develop as they met each week. But that didn't appeal to me. It might feel like a terrific idea to someone else and result in an equally terrific story, but I have to follow my zing.

However, as I began to generate options for what forces them together, I realized I had a second problem. Most women do not want to fall in love with a criminal or see their friends fall in love with them. So not only did these two not have a real reason to spend time together, few readers in their right minds would want them to.

Ugh. My brilliant idea felt like crap. However, I know that this is just how the process works. Ugh doesn't mean the story can't be developed. It means it's in process. And the feeling is just my story sense telling me to fix the issue. On every big story project I've worked on there are always these uncomfortable ugh periods.

So I generated a bunch of ideas to fix those issues, but none of them appealed to me.

Did I give up? No.

When I'm out of options, I know it's time to feed my imagination. I read about coyotes committing rapes and murders, which turned my stomach and made me wonder if I could really use a coyote. I read a couple of interviews with Mexican smugglers. I read up on how coyotes work and found that a lot of it is on a referral basis. You don't want to smuggle someone you don't trust. And you don't want someone smuggling you that you haven't heard good things about. I learned about different legs of the smuggling routes and players involved and how a lot of the smugglers are freelancers and have to pay off the drug cartels for operating in their territory. I read why people come despite the dangers. And about some groups that help them. I also reviewed the descriptions of a probably seventy-five Harlequin romance novels, many of them suspense romances where one or both of the pair was in law enforcement. This all took a number of hours. And there was one point where I just wanted to scrap the idea altogether.

But I trusted the process. Sometimes it's quick. Sometimes it takes a bit longer. While driving, I decided to make use of the time and monkey see monkey adapt some of the ideas I'd seen in those romance novels for what would force my two characters to be together. As I was doing that, a new idea popped into my head. Skydiving. Maybe they are both taking lessons. That would bring them together. I explored the implications a bit and thought, wait, what if he's the instructor?

That was perfect! Suddenly, the music started playing. The idea became electric and began to spawn other ideas. For example, it wasn't Camila, but the grandmother who would be the one to instigate the lessons. And I could see the grandmother being outrageous and sneaky about finding ways to get Camila and Justin together. The skydiving also provided opportunity and reason for Camila and Justin to get close and touch. And after a lesson or two the grandma would talk about Carly and bike riding, and Justin would offer to fix the bike.

At this point, I had an idea that was begging me to write it.

Notice, I didn't say the idea was begging you to write it. I follow my zing; you follow yours. Nor did I say I had an idea that would be a surefire bestseller. Nobody can predict what's going to be a huge seller. Not even publishers. If they could, then every book would be a smashing hit, but they aren't. The best any of us can do is come up with an idea that crackles for us, try our best to make sure it delivers the must-haves for the type of experience we want to offer, and then release that story to readers.

STORY SETUP 2: THE BATTLE OF HARRICK'S VALE

Here's the second expanded story setup. Let's take a look at the elements.

Situation (THOM and Goal)

This is an epic fantasy. It's set at the end of the harvest season in a little village up in Harrick's Vale. Many of the villagers are gone, having traveled out of the mountains to take their livestock and other wares to the big fall market and fair in Lanfael, about three day's travel away. They won't be back for two weeks. Reva, a tough grandmother who is one of the leaders of the village, has stayed behind with a number of others because the delicious, late-season sooch berries are coming on in the hills, and she's not going to leave them to the birds and bears.

The weather's great. The harvest is plentiful, and then two days into it, a gang of village dogs goes missing. They don't show up for breakfast. Don't show up for lunch. A couple of the kids go looking, see a gathering of crows, and find the dog's bodies torn to pieces. They get spooked and flee back to the village.

Reva and the other villagers investigate, but can't see any sign of bear or wolves or even snow lions, which never come this far south anyway. And then Reva's grandson finds a half print of something and a blood trail. But it's not a print any of them recognize.

Reva has a bad feeling about this and sends a rider on the fastest steed to get help, but later that evening the rider's horse comes back by itself, trailing its reins. There's blood on the saddle and on the horse's flanks, and Reva believes the rider was killed.

Something is out there, and Reva and the others are going to need to figure out what it is and how to defeat it before it kills more of them.

Obstacles

There are five men with Reva, some women, and a number of children. Three of the men decide to go hunt the thing. But it kills them. The women are strong, but they're not warriors. And while the last remaining men were once warriors, one is an ancient grandfather and the other lost his leg years ago and is now an ill-kempt drunkard.

Something else that makes this more difficult is that this isn't just some beast or monster come to defend its territory. It's a corom, an intelligent beast, that has been turned into a fell enforcer. It's here for Reva.

Reva comes from a line of pirates. Her grandfather was a pirate king who had made a dark oath with one of the Shaliel, the beings in the world of spirit that grant humans powers in exchange for their service. And that bargain included Reva's service. But Reva rebelled decades ago and refused. A curse fell on her, for the Shaliel's oaths are not to be taken lightly. And the corom is here to finally enforce that oath by taking her grandson. Furthermore, it's not the only one. It will soon be joined by two more.

Characters

I like the five-man band for this: a leader, lancer, heart, smart guy, big guy.

Reva, the Leader

A strong-willed, world-wise, get-er-done village leader. She's in her late forties and is the daughter of a pirate, the granddaughter of a pirate king, and knows well the corrupt dealings of men. She also possesses some small magical powers. She could have greater power, but she utterly refused the service of the Shaliel because she'd rather be poor and free than rich and a slave.

Balstor aka "Blister" aka "The Shark", the Big Guy

Balstor was once the hammer of the king, the king's champion. He was large and fearsome, and men called him The Shark because of his appetite for blood. But then he was injured in a fall from some cliff on an operation conducted at night. Gangrene set in, and he lost his leg. He didn't handle it well and turned to drink. He's now called Blister behind his back.

Morwen, the Lancer

Reva's daughter-in-law who came from another tribe and knows how to use the bow. It's not a war bow; she doesn't have the strength for that. But she's a terrific hunter.

Gramps, the Heart
A wise-cracking grandpa who has a thing for Reva and is also very smart about battle.

Shava, the Smart One
A blunt-speaking, intelligent woman who is incredibly smart with mechanical design. She's bested boat designers, created wooden plumbing, and better bows. She also created a peg leg for Balstor.

Others

- Various kids, including Reva's grandson.
- A couple of other women. I think one will be a big-boned woman. Another might run like the wind. Another might be small.
- Some of the remaining dogs

The Stories

- A story: Reva and team eliminating the threat.
- B story: Balstor becoming the man he can be and regaining his self-respect.
- C story: Reva and Gramps.
- C story: Balstor and Shava.

Magic

The magic consists of certain abilities bestowed upon people by the Shaliel. These abilities can range all over the place: fighting, smithing, moving objects with your mind, summoning lightning, influencing the weather, scrying the future—whatever's cool. It's not going to be magic with tons of rules. However, it does have limitations and costs.

- A person gets only one gift.
- No gift will be so powerful that it could help someone wipe out a city or defeat an army.
- You can only do so much over a short period of time. Do too much and you'll get massive headaches or hallucinations or hypoglycemic effects. If you push too far or try to do something too big, the effort will kill you. It works like a reservoir.
- And the more you use it, the more the Shaliel bind you to do their will.

Reva's pirate king grandfather could summon winds, storms, and lightning. Very handy as a pirate. Her mother could fight with uncanny ability with the sword. She was a notorious pirate. But Reva saw the killings and other injustices the Shaliel required, and decided the gift wasn't worth it. Reva has residual magic from her line. At this point she can lay her hands on someone's eyes and give them enhanced sight, an ability that fades over a number of days. If she were to bind herself to the Shaliel, she could heal and destroy with the touch of her hands. An exceedingly mighty power.

Location

I've decided to use Romania and the Carpathian Mountains as my inspiration for this place. I could have used something in England, Switzerland, Austria, Italy, Turkey, Utah, or a hundred other cool places, but I wanted to take myself to someplace that was new to me. If you google the area, you'll see it gives off a terrific old-world, forest feel. Pointy haystacks, dense forests, white cliffs. You know there are bears in those dark woods. When I get to the outline, I'll do a lot more work on the location. For right now, the pictures and some cursory reading on the place is enough to spark my imagination.

Genre Reminders

Epic fantasy means lots of adventure and discovering magical lore and/or mythical creatures. In mine I want heroes being heroic, facing dilemmas and making the hard, moral choices. I want an "all is lost" moment and a happy ending with a big, satisfying, snatching of victory from the jaws of defeat. There also needs to be great transport to the historical feel and cool Medievalish combat. I also want some big, fun characters.

Setup Brief

- In this epic fantasy
- Reva is a late-forties, good-humored, tough-as-nails leader of a little village up in a mountain vale.
- A few days after most of the village travels to the market, something begins to stalk and kill those that remain.
- Will she be able to save the villagers and her grandson
- When she has nothing but a motley crew of non-fighters; she and the others are trapped in the vale; and the creature begins to call others of its kind to execute an ancient family curse?

Note

This one started as the simple setup of Roxie as Grandma Monster Slayer in chapter four. And that Roxie tale began with her picture, then the genre, then THOM. While this and the Border Love idea started with a picture of a character and the genre, other stories don't.

Please note there's no one right or best sequence for developing each of the elements in a story setup. Start with whatever zing you have. Having said that, I have found that the quicker I identify the genre the easier it is to develop. There's power in making creative decisions, and selecting the genre immediately starts to suggest the types of THOMs, locations, and characters you might use.

When I began to flesh out this setup, I realized that I couldn't give everyone in a whole village a part. There would be too many characters. Also, I wanted a lot of those that could fight to be away because I wanted our group to have the underdog role.

I began thinking of reasons why there would be a small group by themselves in a vale. Maybe they were on patrol. Or a hunt for elk. Or maybe this would be about a group that went out to forage for rare berries in a distant vale and was trapped there. I liked that.

But then I came up with the idea of the market in the big city a few days away. Everyone would want to go, and it would leave just a few behind. And I liked that a little better. A splendid story could be written about a little group going out to hunt elk and running into this creature. But I decided to go with the village.

I also began to wonder why this mythical beast had come to the vale. It could have just been random. There's nothing wrong with that. But I felt I wanted to try some other ideas. So on my daily walk, I did some listing and twisting of ideas. During that walk the idea came into my head that Reva was part of a line of pirates. Maybe her mother or grandmother was a pirate queen. I've always loved the idea of a pirate queen. So I decided to keep that zing.

Another one of the ideas from that walk was the curse. The beast was there for Reva herself. She'd drawn it in. And her previous actions were putting those she loved in jeopardy. I liked that better than the straight monster. There's nothing wrong with a straight monster—a *Jaws* situation. But the one with the curse carried more zing for me, and so I followed that zing trail.

When it was time to create the cast, one of the initial ideas that came to mind was Balstor. I liked the idea of him finding a restoration of his pride and reputation. But I felt like I wanted a few more folks. I went to the five-man band for no other reason than I like that setup. It could have been a two- or three- or four- or seven-person team. I just happened to like the bigger size and types in the five. Reva, of course, was the leader. Balstor could be the big guy. I then began to fill in the blanks for the others.

The smart one was originally Reva's grandson. But there was something about having him in the lineup that just didn't feel right. My writer's sense was acting up. I can't tell you any reason why—he just didn't excite me; I wasn't interested in him participating. I'm sure another writer could have written a fabulous tale with him.

I looked at the other minor female characters that might be there—the big-framed one and lightning fast one—and really liked the idea of making most of these characters women. In fact, I toyed with the idea of making them all women. But I wanted Balstor there. And so I decided to turn Shavis into Shava. Because this was the role for the smart one, I immediately thought of a character I loved in Anthony Ryan's Bloodsong series that I read this summer and decided to let Ryan's character inspire this one.

As for the magic, I didn't want a big complicated set of rules. I wanted to keep it mystical. Someone else could have come up with a more defined magic system and written a brilliant story. But I was feeling more zing for this one, and so I went with single abilities. And because of the curse, I decided that there would be some beings or demons or something on the other side that would be granting these, but for a price.

Do I know how Reva will resolve this issue? No. I have absolutely no idea. However, because the THOM is centered in the magic, I'm thinking the solution must be there too. Maybe there will be some lore she discovers in some old book she has, or something she remembers from her mother, or maybe she has an amulet her mother gave her. Maybe Balstor knows of something from one of his old travels. Or maybe Shava has some insight. I'm not sure. I have no idea what the solution is at this point. What I do know is that I have a story setup that has gotten me excited and is begging me to write it. Later, as I develop the outline, I'll figure the ending out.

A FEW THINGS TO THINK ABOUT

First of all, I hope you noticed that the second story setup takes a slightly different form than the first. I did that on purpose to illustrate that what's important are the setup elements, not the format they're presented in.

Next, both of these stories featured strong female characters. Am I

Create Story Ideas that Beg to be Written

suggesting that all great ideas need females as the main characters? No. That's just where my zing happened to take me. Follow your zing.

Third, I ran into story snags during the development of both of these ideas. Sometimes you'll get an idea that develops easily. But, more often than not, snags are part of the process. All writers run into story snags or story problems that seem to defy us. What will set you apart as a writer is how you approach them. All of the key principles and tools that I've found helpful for dealing with snags are in this book. Use them.

Fourth, did you notice that summaries of the story setups for these stories aren't long? The summary for *Border Love* is about 1,100 words. The summary for *The Battle of Harrick's Vale* is 1,200 words.

Why aren't these longer? Why don't I have extensive character backstories for the core characters, or even list all the characters involved? Why don't I nail down the dominant impressions for all the locations? Why don't I detail more about the magic in Reva's story? I've left a lot of unanswered questions.

First, I don't need an extensive character backstory. They don't seem to help me much. You may find yours are longer. There isn't a perfect size.

Second, this is a story setup. It's the concept, the story engine, not the whole car or the journey.

Third, I've found it's impossible to know everything up front. Many story questions don't arise until after I've made various creative decisions, and we're making creative decisions until we finish the project. Each of those decisions can prompt questions that you never could have foreseen way back when you were first developing the setup. So I don't expect to know it all up front.

Fourth, the creative process I'm sharing with you is a three-step process that starts with big structure elements and then adds in more and more detail. The first step is to develop a rough concept (the story setup). You then add more detail with the outline. And then you finish with the actual chapters—the specific things the characters say, do, think, and feel.

However, writing is not like building a house from a blueprint—you don't create a blueprint for the story with every detail you need and then simply assemble it. You develop the story as you go, adding detail until you finish. That's part of the joy of writing stories—you're surprising yourself all the way to the end.

Furthermore, the steps in the process often overlap. Events and incidents in the plot presented themselves to me while developing each of the setups above. I've shared a few of those events in the summaries. So I'm already getting some of what may end up in the outlines.

But it's not just one way. Working through the outline will give me ideas about the story setup. It will spark ideas that will deepen elements in the setup, but it might also prompt me to change some of the core setup elements. And this will continue when I write the chapters.

Most of the changes will be small and work within the structure of the setup, but sometimes I've developed an idea and outline only to find when I begin to write the chapters that it doesn't work. It doesn't fit the characters. Or maybe things don't work that way in real life. Or I suddenly get a megawatt zing that changes everything. Either way, I have to go back and adjust.

Even with such adjustments, I've found that this saves gobs of time. Working from sketch to draft allows you to try lots and lots of options up front so you can nail down the big elements quickly. You don't want to spend the time writing a whole novel only to come to the end and realize the basic concept doesn't work. I did that once with a nice, fat 230,000-word epic fantasy that was on contract. Months and months of work scrapped. And it could have all been avoided if I had just taken the time to develop a story setup that made sense and crackled with electricity first.

16

WHAT'S NEXT?

The process I'm sharing with you has these three steps:

- Develop a story setup
- Develop an outline
- Write the chapters

You've now come to the end of the book on the story setup. What's your next step?

Well, it's to go and develop the setups for a whole bunch of stories. And have fun while you're doing it.

Please remember that there's no one right sequence for developing the elements of your story setup. You can start with setting, character, THOM, or obstacle. You can start with a name, an incident, story turn, or ending. You can start anywhere. Stories build like a snowball with a bit of snow added here and a bit of snow added there. This means you'll most likely move back and forth between the elements. However, I will recommend that you nail down the genre as quickly as possible. I have found that greatly speeds the development.

After you've developed all of the key elements for a bunch of setups, you'll have a number of concepts that attract you. That means you'll be in the enviable position of getting to choose from a bunch of ideas that beg you to write them.

Select that story concept you want to run with the most and move to the next step. I recommend going through the process of sketching an outline, which is what the next book with cover. It's a terrific way to develop the events of the story. Furthermore, it's just a sketch. If something is not quite right, you're not out weeks or months of detailed work. You can toss it and easily create another and another until you've got something hot in your hands. And you can change them as you go. These sketches act as first drafts of the story and can be a lot of fun.

However, if you don't want to go through that process, then don't. Be happy and go write your chapters.

Either way, I hope to see your tales delight and move your audience. Good luck!

APPENDIX A: STORY SETUP CHECKLIST

Here's a checklist of key things to think about while developing the setup for your story. Develop until you find that interesting situation. Those interesting characters. And the stakes and obstacles that promise a struggle.

Genre

- What are the vicarious thrills and satisfactions my readers come to these types of stories for?
- What types of characters, places, events, and situations do I and other readers come to this genre for?
- What mandatory experiences must I include?
- How is this experience going to be the same, but also enjoyably different?
- What segments of the market for this genre am I not targeting?

Compelling Character

Questions About the Hero

Appendix A: Story Setup Checklist

- Is this someone the reader can root for?
- Do I feel the character crackling with electricity?
- Is this someone my audience will want to spend hours with?
- Does this character have key attributes heroes need?
- Have I added something that will humanize this character?

Questions About the Antagonist

- Is this someone the reader can root against?
- What's this person's goal?
- How is this person a formidable adversary?
- Does this character have key attributes antagonists need?

Questions About All Major Characters

- Do I have a sketch?
- Does the sketch give me a clear idea of the character?
- Does the character have some zing to them?

Questions About the Cast

- Do I have too many characters?
- Are all of my characters different?
- Am I enjoying this cast? Does it crackle with electricity?

Awesome THOM and Goal

- What's the main THOM of this story?
- Will the stakes be high enough for my readers to care?
- What's the reason why the hero can't or won't just walk away?
- What's the specific thing the hero wants to gain or retain?
- What's surprising with this situation?
- Does the THOM and goal crackle with electricity for me?

Formidable Obstacle

Appendix A: Story Setup Checklist

- What's the big obstacle?
- Is the hero an underdog?
- Is the obstacle formidable?
- Can I see some ways the difficulties might increase as the story progresses?
- Can I feel that this promises a struggle?

Cool Locations

- What's cool, fun, or interesting in this location?
- What could give the hero trouble in the efforts to reach the goal?
- What's the dominant impression of the place?

Multiple Storylines

- If I have additional storylines, what are they?
- Is this going to take an A/A/A or an A/B/C structure?
- Is this part of a series? If so, will any of the storylines span more than this book?

APPENDIX B: FANTASY AND SCIENCE FICTION

Some tips on developing magic, sci-fi technology, and mythical or alien creatures for your stories.

MAGIC

There are five things that seem to make magic systems come alive. And they're all related to, surprise surprise, the principles you've already learned. However, before we get into the five elements, I want to remind you about the creative principles you learned earlier. I want you to especially remember the principles of "Monkey See, Monkey Adapt" and "Follow the Rule of Cool." That means you won't worry about coming up with a magic system that's nothing like anything anybody has ever seen before. Because there's nothing out there that hasn't been influenced by something else.

For example, look at all the different vampire stories that have found success. Some use the trope of passing the vampiric power down through the family line. Others use the trope of a nasty virus as the source. Others use the trope of a curse. Yet others use the idea that a super-secret sci-fi serum (probably first tested by the Nazis) creates vampires. They're all common tropes. And readers love 'em.

So don't worry about being wholly original. Instead, focus on the rule of cool and coming up with some twist (even if it's a small one) with the abilities, sources, applications, limitations, ramifications, risks, complications, lore, mystery, or secrets of your magic.

Or don't come up with a twist to the magic.

Sometimes it's more than enough to simply present a familiar magic with a different set of characters, problems, or places. For example, maybe your vampiric lore is fairly traditional, but your little twist is that the vampires are redneck trailer trash. Or maybe they're rabbits, aliens, Victorians, or some lost tribe in the Amazon.

Or maybe, instead of being supernatural monsters, your vampires play a different role. They're heroes, super soldiers, vagabonds, detectives, or do-gooder grannies.

Or maybe you switch the genre and put them in a Western, space opera, American Civil War story, spy story, comedy, or Scottish time-travel romance.

Use the tropes you love. Twist them or some other aspect of the story. The possibilities are endless. Your goal is to just have fun.

So what are the five things that make magic come alive? Where will your brainstorming probably be most productive? Here's number one.

What It Does

Your readers love magic is because it allows them to think about having cool powers and doing cool things with it. It's an attractive fantasy. It's wish-fulfillment. For example, wouldn't it be exciting to be able to do all of these things?

- Talk to animals
- Have super strength
- Breathe under water
- Communicate by thought
- Summon a cheeky goblin to help you defeat bad guys
- Animate a little man made out of willow to stand guard while you sleep

We also love these things about magic itself:

- Learning the details of a lore, including different classes and types of magic and magic users
- Discovering a lost and ancient lore or powerful artifact
- The feeling of mystery and secrets

You may have other things you love about magic. The point is to follow the rule of cool when developing yours. So when you're developing magic, ask yourself these questions:

- What cool, scary, funny, mysterious, or thrilling things can my magic do?
- How does it work–what's the lore?
- What things are not yet explained or known?
- Has anything been lost?
- Are there any cool mysteries or secrets?

The first principle is to explore what you think would be fun and cool.

How You Access It

The next thing is to think about is where the magic comes from. I list some common sources below. Review them, and start generating ideas for the ones that interest you.

Possess a Cool Ability

Some characters simply possess a magical ability. You see this with comic book characters like the X-Men, the characters on the TV series *Heroes*, the elves in *Lord of the Rings*, and the allomancers in the Mistborn series that can burn metals to magical effect. You see this when someone has the powers of lycanthropy, can fly like Superman, or is part of a family that has magic in the blood or DNA.

Harness a General Power in the Environment

Sometimes the power is simply in the environment and acts like elec-

Appendix B: Fantasy and Science Fiction

tricity or some other natural resource. So you access the Force in the Star Wars universe, or Sadin and Sadar in The Wheel of Time series. Or you harness things like the power of the sun, moon, ley lines, earthsense, etc. The power source is out there. Your job is to learn how to find it, tap into it, and use it in cool ways.

Transfer and Use Power Possessed by Something Else
Sometimes the power is possessed by someone or something else, and you need to transfer it from them to you. Maybe you steal an attribute like beauty or strength from someone else. Maybe the power is in the blood of people born with magical abilities, and you steal that. Maybe you simply steal their life force. It can be a general or specific type of power. If a sentient being possesses it, the power can be stolen or given. If the power is in an object, you frequently extract or consume it like you might the petals of a rare flower, the sap of a certain tree, or the juices of a dragon.

Control Someone or Something That Can Wield Magic
Sometimes, instead of wielding the power yourself, you control or influence a creature or person that has the power to wield it for you. Examples of this include summoning, binding, enslaving, or making pacts with genies, demons, elementals, fairies, furies, etc. So maybe you can't do the deed, but the goblin you control can.

Use an Object of Power
In this method, some object holds the power, and what you need to do is possess the object and learn how to wield it. So you might wield a wand, ring, amulet, talisman, staff, magical thigh bone, elf stone, etc.

Employ a Lore That Creates the Magic
All of the methods above deal with powers that already exist. But you can also create magic by performing some, usually arcane, act. This includes things like mixing potions, reciting incantations, drawing runes, forming hexes, weaving certain patterns, singing songs of power, etc.

Mixes

Finally, you can mix and match the methods above. So you might need to recite a specific incantation to imbue a sword with power, summon a wraith, or bestow an ability on someone. Or you might transfer some general source of power into a talisman that allows you affect the weather. Or you might have the special ability to learn the lore of creating paper origami servants like we see in Holmberg's *The Paper Magician*.

What Its Limitations Are

The third thing you want to think about is that magic is basically the fantasy equivalent of technology. It's a tool to help with a problem such as winning a battle, healing someone, spying, etc. It allows you to do things faster or better. Or accomplish things you couldn't otherwise.

For example, if you want to defeat a thug that's trying to steal your money, you could fight him with your fists, or you could use some incantation to make him fall asleep. If you need to scale a castle wall, you could use a grapple hook and rope, or you could use a talisman that gives you the power to bound like a flea to the crenellations. Magic is just a different way of accomplishing a task. An exciting way.

However, you need to make sure you don't give your main character so much power you essentially remove all obstacles from your character's path. Remember that your readers want to hope and fear for the character. And they can't do that if your main character is so powerful that nothing can stand in his or her way or touch those they care about. You need to put limits on the power. When you do, those limits make the magic and story much more interesting.

How do you limit the power? There are a bunch of ways.

Give It a Mind of Its Own

The first way is to give the magic a mind of its own. For example, the cheeky goblin you summon might interpret your commands in passive-aggressive ways or flat out refuse to do certain things. Or maybe the magic you have is on loan from some entity, and you have to live a certain way to access it. Or maybe the magic force has its own agenda and comes and goes according to what its goals are. Maybe it's ornery.

Limit the Size of the Effect
Another option is to limit the magnitude, duration, or distance of your power. For example, maybe your mind control power can't compel anyone; it can only whisper suggestions. Or maybe you have to be up close and can only compel people you're touching. Or maybe your compulsion only lasts for a few minutes. If your power allows you to control the weather, maybe you can affect the temperature within a hundred feet, but you can't change the weather over a large area. Or maybe you can affect a larger area, but only for a brief time. Furthermore, maybe you can only affect the weather where you are physically located—you can't affect the weather on the other side of the globe.

Limit the Number of Abilities
A third option is to limit the number of abilities a person might have. For example, in your world, there might be a dozen (or a hundred) special abilities, but each person only gets one. Or maybe only a rare few get any ability at all.

Use a Finite Fuel
A fourth way to limit the power is to require that it use a finite fuel. For example, maybe there's some rare plant that fuels it, and when it's used up, it's gone. Or maybe the fuel comes in the form of some rare magical liquid. Or maybe it's generated by unicorn berries, and, well, you haven't found any unicorn poop for a long time. In a similar way, maybe the magic costs something dear. For example, maybe every time you use it, you lose a day from your life. Or memories. Or maybe it cripples you bit by bit. Or maybe it sickens someone close to you.

Make It Hard to Learn
A sixth way to limit the power is to require the knowledge of some lore to produce it. And make that lore hard to learn, and so it takes years or decades to master it.

Beef Up the Opposition
Another way to avoid overpowering your characters is to is to give the opposition greater abilities. Or give them powers that counter or undermine your character's ability. So maybe your character is an apprentice mage, but the villain is a full-blown, level ten mage that can command an army of golems. Or maybe your character can crush automobiles with his mind, but the villain's henchwoman put a collar on his neck that controls him.

You Don't Need to Use Every Limitation Known to Man (or Woman)
Please note that you don't have to use all of the methods listed above. Gandalf's magic in *The Lord of the Rings* didn't cost him anything. It didn't have a mind of its own. And no finite fuel was involved. His power was simply limited in magnitude—he wasn't strong enough to overpower every enemy or obstacle that stood in his path. He had a simple limitation, yet Gandalf was super cool. So your goal isn't to develop a limitation in every category. It's to simply develop a limitation you think is cool.

Risks and Complications of Using It

The fourth thing that can make your magic fun and fresh are the risks it brings. Is the magic unstable? Does it produce unwanted side effects? Can it turn on you? What happens if it does? In short, what could go wrong?

For example, it might be super risky to summon a fury to do your bidding. As risky as riding a river with class 6 rapids. If you're not vigilant, it will turn on you. Or enslave you. Or strike someone close to you.

If you look at *The Lord of the Rings*, the one ring carried the risk of revealing your location to Sauron, calling to one of the Nine, and turning you into a Gollum-like creature.

Or maybe there's some complication. Magic is like technology. So maybe your amulet is the equivalent of a junky car. And just as a junky car might let you down by not always starting, maybe your amulet is old and half-broken and doesn't always work. Or maybe it creates some kind of magical exhaust that chokes you and makes you cough. Or maybe, just as a clunker car might have super soft brakes that might fail at any time, so too your amulet might have some ward on it that fails while you're using it and sends your magic careening off in some weird direction.

Risks and complications are fun, fruitful ground.

How It Impacts Your World

The fifth big thing that provides lots of cool ideas is thinking about the impact the very existence of the magic has on your world. One little invention can have an impact on so many things.

For example, look at the impact of the airplane. You could suddenly transport goods faster. You could transport people the same way. You could get a view of things on the ground like you couldn't before. Because of this, almost as soon as airplanes were invented, they were used to drop bombs on people. And shoot people from the sky. And spy. They helped businesses, travelers, researchers, search and rescue teams, people who needed specialized medical care, drug traffickers, snow skiers, and on and on. New businesses and vocations arose. New supply chains. New entertainments. New dangers.

Your magic will have a similar impact. So start by thinking about what specific tasks in the society the magic can be used for. Would it help in baking, carrying the king's messages, making clothes, fishing, programming computers, making pizza, waging war, enhancing your attractiveness, perpetrating crimes, enforcing the law, spying, transporting food, growing crops, treating sickness and injuries—or any other task? Magic is like technology, so what might they use this technology for? You don't have to write an encyclopedia on every possible application. Just follow your zing.

You will then want to think about the consequences, the ramifications, of using it for those tasks.

For example, if you use magic in you baking business, what effect might that have on competitors, buyers, your staff, your dog that eats the scraps, or the urchin that filches pies? Does it change how you're trained? Does it affect the environment? Does it make people fear the baker will do something to them? If so, what do they do to make themselves feel safe?

Just take some time to think about who or what else it might affect. And the effect that will have. And maybe even the effect that effect will have. And maybe even the effect of the effect of the effect. Heck, as you follow your zing, maybe you'll find that pirates in your world don't want to steal gold coins—they want to steal the hard tack biscuits sent to magically fortify the king's army.

What you'll use the magic for and how that impacts people, society, the environment, animals, etc. is such rich ground for finding what's cool.

Let's look at another example. Let's say you can conjure winds. What could you do with that, and what impact would that have?

Well, you might be able to sail larger or faster ships. And larger and faster ships will allow you to dominate as a pirate or sea power. Or maybe you don't want to be a pirate—maybe you want to smuggle all sorts of stuff across the seas.

Maybe you rig up some land vehicle powered by wind. And that might lead to massive road building. And some new vocations like wind driver or wind mechanic.

Maybe you could use wind to blow sand, dirt, or glass into the eyes of an enemy army. Or blow some poisonous smoke their way. Maybe it could help you fling arrows or send them off course. That means the opposing force would want to seek your wind wizards out and kill them. And devise other counter measures.

Maybe you can use the wind to blow some kind of crazy horn that deafens people. Or maybe it whispers things in the woods. Or blows messages across long distances, replacing carrier pigeons with magical zephyrs. Maybe it allows you to create bigger windmills.

What kind of an effect would these things have on society? Maybe if you have this power, you can sell your services to a local king or duke. Or maybe that local king thinks your kind poses a threat, and so he tests all children for the gift and takes them into his service. Maybe other kings send secret agents to find the gifted in your kingdom and assassinate them or kidnap them. Or maybe the wind blowers unite and take over the kingdom. Or maybe they flee to the northern reaches and build their own kingdom. Or maybe their numbers are so few they don't have enough to build a kingdom, but can create a hideout. And maybe they waylay rich folks and steal their goods, hence the name windthief or windrobber.

One magic idea can spawn tons of cool ideas. One idea can be all you need to spawn an awesome world. Take some time to explore the applications and ramifications of the magic on your world.

Common or Rare

As you develop your magic system, it can be helpful to step back for a moment and get an idea of how much magic you want in your world. Sometimes we stuff our stories with so much magic that it becomes window dressing. And sometimes that's cool. The Harry Potter books were that way. You couldn't walk anywhere in that world without encountering something magical. The world was saturated in magic. And readers loved it.

But you can also have a wonderful story where magic is much less common. For example, if you think about the prevalence of magic in *The Lord of the Rings*, you'll see there was a lot less of it than in *Harry Potter*. The one ring really only gave Frodo the power to disappear. He couldn't use it to fly, blast orcs, or produce second breakfast.

Gandalf didn't do much that was magical either. He produced magical light and fireworks. He could communicate with moths and counter Suraman's spell that possessed Theoden. But what else did Gandalf's magic really do? Gandalf mostly knew a lot of history and spoke a lot of languages. I think the draw of Tolkien's story focused much more on adventure—on meeting mythical beings like dragons, elves, orcs, and giant eagles and going to mythical places like Rivendell, Minas Tirith, and Mordor.

So don't feel like you must have a certain level of magic in your stories. You can have a lot or a little or something in between. Follow your zing. Do what you think is cool.

SCI-FI TECHNOLOGY

Guess what? Technology in most science fiction works like magic. That means all the principles above apply to space ships, robots, and artificial intelligence.

One thing you'll want to think about is how much you want to explain the science behind your tech. In some science fiction stories, the author treats the tech like a black box. It just does what it does without needing much explanation. There was a lot of this in the original *Star Trek*. And readers and viewers loved it. We didn't need to know the science behind a tricorder any more than we need to know the science behind how cell phones or satellites actually work. They just work, and it's cool.

In other stories, the authors geek out using current science to imagine what might be possible in the future. Michael Crichton did this in a number of his books. You can see it in *Jurassic Park* where he takes what we know about DNA and imagines what cool and dangerous thing might be possible with dinosaurs. Andy Weir did this in *The Martian* as well, extrapolating current science to see how you could survive when stranded on Mars.

You'll want to give some thought to the ramifications of whatever new tech you introduce. For example, what's the ramification on battle if you can accelerate large objects to a gazillion miles an hour. If you can do that, you can turn a boulder into a massive kinetic weapon, something equivalent to a nuclear weapon. What kinds of attacks and defenses would that produce?

You'll also want to consider the realities of physics and biology and how they might affect things. For example, can an explosion make sound in the vacuum of space? How will that change the way people experience battles in that environment? People lose muscle and bone strength when they live in weightless environments. What kind of effect will that have on your people?

Read all the science and tech you can, including projections of what's coming in the future. You'll find a lot of fun story gold there. But realize you can't know it all, and at some point you just have to go with what you know, use some black boxes and hand-wavium, and have fun.

Appendix B: Fantasy and Science Fiction

CREATURES

Very often, both fantasy and science fiction stories include awesome creatures. Mythical creatures in fantasy. Wonderous alien life in science fiction. Are you interested in having any in your world? If so, list them out. Then answer these questions about them:

- What makes them cool, scary, funny, mysterious, or thrilling?
- Do they have any powers? If so, what are they? And what are their limitations?
- What are the ramifications of having these creatures in the world?

Do you want them to be more than mysterious? If so, you probably want to explore the biology and sociology of the creatures.

Biology includes things like how they reproduce, how they are born and die, what they eat, what makes them sick, how they heal, how they move and where they live, what they can perceive, and what environmental (or dimensional) niche they live in.

Sociology includes things like whether they are solitary or communal, how they organize themselves (families, tribes, nations?), their types and ethnicities, how they govern their societies, what they value, who some of the majorities and minorities are in their societies, their enemies and allies, what they consider criminal or disgusting, what they think is admirable, what their language is, whether they have any religions, and how this manifests in their culture.

Remember that you're not trying to write an encyclopedia about them. You're just trying to generate some zing. And these areas are good zing-hunting grounds.

HOW TO USE MAGIC AND TECH AS A SOURCE FOR STORY IDEAS

You can do more with magic and tech than create stuff that's cool. You can use them to develop your story setup and plot. Remember the THOM? Threats and hardships establish story questions. And a very productive way to come up with those is to ask what could go wrong in a given situation. So what could go wrong with someone possessing some magic or technology? What perils might that introduce?

Could the ability to whisper thoughts into people's minds introduce the opportunity for the abuse of power?

Could nanotechnology get out of control and pose a massive threat?

What could go wrong with bringing dinosaurs back?

Or dragons?

Michael Crichton and Robert J. Sawyer made careers out of looking at a technology and asking that question. Don't hesitate to follow their examples in your science fiction or fantasy genre.

Another part of the THOM is presenting an opportunity for the character to do, be, or possess something awesome.

For example, every book that's about a kid becoming a magician's apprentice or going to magic school is about that attractive fantasy. Every book about battle robots is about that attractive fantasy. So ask yourself what the cool opportunity could be?

Another part of the THOM is mystery. How many fantasy stories include discovering a lost lore? How many sci-fi stories are about discovering some new or lost technology? You can use this too. Just ask yourself what cool thing you could make a mystery.

USING REAL LIFE AS A SOURCE FOR WORLD BUILDING

I want to share one last tip that can save you a ton of time. World building, while fun, can distract you from your goal. You want to write stories, not spend all your time developing encyclopedia articles on the climate, history, geography, culture, technology, flora, fauna, language, and dozens of other topics about a place and time. At the same time, the more you know about a place, the easier it is to get ideas for characters, story setup elements, and plots. So what do you do?

One way to make your life easier is by using a real physical place or society to inspire your imaginary one. That real place or society already has all of the details. All you need to do is learn some of the basics, then make some tweaks for your story.

You can use real-life geographies and peoples. For example, Orson

Appendix B: Fantasy and Science Fiction

Card based his Alvin Maker series on North America in the 1800s. Jim Butcher used the Roman legions as an inspiration for his Codex Alera series. Larry Correia used India for his Forgotten Warrior series. John Flanagan used Western Europe to inspire his Ranger's Apprentice and Brotherband series. I set my Dark God series in a geography stolen from Boston and a climate stolen from northern California.

You can also use real-world stories and conflicts to help you come up with THOMs in your fantasy or sci-fi world. For example, George R.R. Martin used the real-world conflicts in the War of Roses to inspire his popular Song of Fire and Ice series. Joss Whedon used Western tropes in his sci-fi TV series *Serenity*.

You can even use real-world organizations. Maybe your magic is taught in a system like that of the old English boarding schools (hmm, sounds suspiciously like Harry Potter), the US Navy SEALS, the construction industry, or the old Japanese samurai. Maybe your magical powers are based on quantum mechanics or biological processes or the forces you learn about in physics.

Finally, focus your research of real life on the things that will affect your story. If the story is about a war between two mercenary guilds, learn about guilds and mercenaries. But don't feel like you need to go research the pests farmers have to deal with on their crops. If a number of scenes take place on a ship, go research ships and sailing. But don't feel you need to create a 1,000-year history of sailing in your world.

The bottom line is that you can find great ideas and save yourself some time by looking at the real world and using the principle of monkey see, monkey adapt.

DEAR READER

I hope you found the insights in the book useful.

If you did, please leave a review on Amazon.

Not only will it help fellow readers, it will also help me bring you more books, including the next one in the series.

READ MORE BY JOHN D. BROWN

Action, Adventure, and Characters You Want to Cheer For

For epic fantasy lovers:

The Drovers Series

The Dark God Series

For those who enjoy thrillers:

The Frank Shaw Series

If you're interested in the Novel Writers Academy, join John's newsletter to keep up-to-date on future releases and receive exclusive bonus content.

www.johndbrown.com

ACKNOWLEDGMENTS

A big thanks goes to **Alan Gorevan**, **Anthony Lazendic**, **Ashley Ghere**, **Chris Clark**, **Lyn Worthen**, **Pieter Jongejans**, **Stephen Wein** for super helpful beta reads of an early draft. Another thanks goes to **Kelli Ann Morgan** for her skills and patience while working with me on the cover. Finally, **Alexandria Wall** and **Nellie Brown** have provided invaluable support for the whole academy idea. Without their help, I would never had been able to make the time.

ABOUT JOHN

John D. Brown is the bestselling author of the The Drovers series, The Dark God series, and the Frank Shaw series. He lives in the hinterlands of Utah where there's lots of fresh air, many good-hearted ranchers, and a redtailed hawk that likes to occasionally dive bomb him on his hikes.

Learn more about John at his website.

If you liked this book, please take a minute to leave a review. It will help the author bring you more books.

Made in United States
Orlando, FL
20 April 2022

17002835R20129